Modeling
With NLP

by

Robert B. Dilts

Meta Publications
P.O. Box 1910
Capitola, California 95010
(408) 464-0254
FAX (408) 464-0517

Library of Congress Card Number 98-06-62 87
I.S.B.N. 0-916990-41-9

Contents

iii

Dedication

This book is dedicated with much love and respect to:
Judith DeLozier
Todd Epstein
Gino Bonissone
Tim Hallbom
Suzi Smith
Robert McDonald
Richard Clarke
Stephen Gilligan
David Gordon
Leslie Cameron-Bandler
John Grinder
Richard Bandler
and all of my other co-modelers who have helped make NLP such a rich field of endeavor.

Acknowledgments

I would like to acknowledge:

Judith DeLozier, who contributed tremendously to the sections in this book on Modeling and NLP. She has been a constant inspiration and a wonderful working partner throughout the more than twenty years that we have known each other.

David Gordon and the late Todd Epstein, two of the most committed modelers I have known. They both possess a remarkable ability to balance rigor with curiosity, and, as a result, ask *great* questions. They have helped me to develop much greater insight and clarity to my understanding of the modeling process.

John Grinder and Richard Bandler for originating the methodology and approach upon which this work is based, and for demonstrating the incredible power of modeling.

Gino Bonissone and Ivanna Gasperini, my mentors and research assistants in the leadership project from which the second part of this book is drawn. Their committed efforts, creative contributions, and unwavering support made the project a success.

Gianfranco Gambigliani, who, as Chief Executive Officer of ISVOR Fiat, had the courage and foresight to sponsor the leadership study upon which a substantial part of this book is based.

Giovanni Testa, who guided the implementation of the leadership research project, and has continued to support the mission that this book represents for so many years.

All of the leaders who participated in the study. Their wisdom and skill has been an inspiration to me in ways they will never realize.

Ami Sattinger, who helped with the proof reading and editing of this book. She has been one of my most important resources as a writer.

Preface

My passion for modeling began nearly twenty-five years ago when I first met John Grinder and Richard Bandler. They had just finished the first volume of their groundbreaking work, *The Structure of Magic* (1975), in which they had modeled the language patterns and intuitions of three of the world's most effective psychotherapists. Their model allowed a person such as myself, a third year political science major at the University of California at Santa Cruz, who had no personal experience with therapy of any type, to ask questions that an experienced therapist might ask.

I had come in contact with John Grinder as a result of attending one of his classes on linguistics, and actually had very little interest in therapy at that point. I found myself, however, awed and excited about the potential practical applications of the modeling approach. It seemed to me that modeling had important implications in all areas of human endeavor: politics, the arts, management, science, teaching, and so on.

I found the modeling approach to be a perfect blending of theory and practice, and of intuition and understanding. It struck me that the methodology of modeling could lead to broad innovations in many fields, and help create access to a great deal of untapped potential for people of all types.

As a student of political philosophy, my own first "modeling project" was to apply the linguistic filters that Grinder and Bandler had used in their analysis of psychotherapists to see what patterns might emerge from studying the Socratic dialogs of Plato (*Plato's Use of the Dialectic in The Republic: A Linguistic Analysis*, Fall, 1975). A more in depth study of people like Socrates, Karl Marx, Abraham Lincoln, Mahatma Gandhi, Adolph Hitler, and Jesus of Nazareth, lead me to formalize what I called Sleight of Mouth Patterns - language patterns by which beliefs could be verbally established, reframed, and transformed.

My next applications of modeling were in the field of education. Projects included the study of effective spelling, typing, accelerated reading, and other learning strategies, which formed the basis of an approach to education that I termed "Dynamic Learning." Some of the results of these studies included computer software (*Spelling Strategy*, *Math Strategy* and *Typing Strategy*, 1982) and a seminar package described in the book *Dynamic Learning* (co-authored with Todd Epstein, 1995).

My mother's reoccurrence of breast cancer in the early 1980's (and her dramatic recovery, assisted by NLP processes) lead me to model patterns of effective health and healing, and the influence of beliefs and belief systems on both mental and physical health. This resulted in patterns such as Reimprinting, Integration of Conflicting Beliefs, the Belief Change Cycle, Neuro-Logical Levels, and the Allergy Technique; described in *Changing Belief Systems with NLP* (1990) and *Beliefs: Pathways to Health and Well Being* (co-authored with Tim Hallbom and Suzi Smith, 1990).

Other modeling projects included research into strategies for creativity and innovation, resulting in *Tools for Dreamers* (co-authored with Todd Epstein, 1991). In the series *Strategies of Genius Vols. I, II & III* (1994-1995), I applied the tools of NLP to model the thinking processes of important historical figures; such as Aristotle, Sir Arthur Conan Doyle's Sherlock Holmes, Walt Disney, Mozart, Albert Einstein, Sigmund Freud, Leonardo da Vinci and Nikola Tesla.

As this list of projects implies, modeling is the generative core of NLP. Yet, aside from some comments I have provided about eliciting strategies in *Tools for Dreamers*, *Dynamic Learning* and *Strategies of Genius*, no comprehensive account of the modeling process has actually appeared in any NLP book to date. The goal of the first part of this book is to describe the key principles, procedures and strategies of the NLP modeling process. The second part of the book illustrates how NLP modeling procedures and distinctions have been applied to the examination of the complex subject of leadership.

In 1988 I began an extensive study of leadership skills based on the principles and distinctions of Neuro-Linguistic Programming. The study included interviews and interactions with top managers in organizations throughout Europe and the United States. *Visionary Leadership Skills* (1996), the companion volume to this book, describes a number of the strategies and techniques resulting from this project.

A main stimulus for this study was my introduction to Gino Bonissone, a consultant working in the areas of strategy formulation and organizational development, in Milan. Gino, a man of remarkable intelligence and energy, and more than thirty years my senior, recognized the tremendous potential of NLP in the area of organizational change. In each other, we also found a remarkable combination of shared interests and complementary skills. Through time we were to become each other's mentors, students, colleagues and ultimately co-developers with respect to the applications of NLP to organizational leadership and change. The book *Skills for the Future* (1993) is one product of our continuing collaboration.

One of our first projects together was a study of effective leadership skills, sponsored by Fiat in Italy. This project proved to be a major contribution to my larger leadership study. The project was sponsored by Gianfranco Gambigliani and Giovanni Testa at ISVOR Fiat; two men who possessed a brilliance, commitment and foresight that continues to impress me to this day. The second half of this book describes both the process and results of that modeling project.

While the substance of this study was rooted in the examination of leadership in organizations and companies, the applications of the skills described are relevant to many situations.

They can be an invaluable resource for people interested or involved in group and organizational work of any kind, whether it is related to management, consulting, organizational development, training, teaching, or even parenting.

The skills of modeling and leadership have transformed my life both personally and professionally. I hope you find these skills equally valuable in transforming yourself, in whichever direction you would like to move.

Robert Dilts
Santa Cruz, California
April, 1998

Introduction

Thomas Jefferson once said, "If two individuals get together and exchange a dollar, they each walk away with one dollar. If the same individuals get together and exchange an idea, they both walk away with *two* ideas." In many ways, this statement expresses the vastly generative potential or "economics" of modeling.

Modeling is essentially a process of "sharing ideas." The ability to model effectively opens the door to many possibilities that have previously been unavailable to humankind. In addition to providing a methodology which can be used to make ideas more explicit and easier to communicate, modeling can transform the way we view and perceive one another.

If we see someone who does something better than ourselves, for example, instead of looking at that person and feeling inadequate, jealous, or suspicious, we can go out and model how they do what they do. Then, we too can have the capability that the other person possesses. Rather than take something away from that person, both we and the other person are able to benefit: we by acquiring a new capability, and the other person, by having better understanding and conscious competence with respect to his or her skills. Many others also can benefit as a result of having access to a valuable capability that has been modeled.

There is an old adage which states that "if you give a person a fish, you have fed him for a day; but if you teach a person how to fish, you have fed him for the rest of his life." The value of helping someone to 'model' an effective fisherman would be that it would involve (a) helping that person to get his or her fish for the day, and in doing so, (b) teaching the person how to fish – a skill that will last the person the rest of his or her life. Thus, modeling involves achieving two simultaneous outcomes – getting a particular result, and, at the same time, learning explicitly how to do it. It is this feature that makes modeling one of the most powerful forms of "learning to learn" that is available.

This book is about the NLP modeling process and its application to the study of effective leadership abilities. The first part of this book is devoted to defining the principles and tools necessary for effective modeling (the "epistemology," methodology and technology of NLP). *Modeling* is the process of taking a complex event or phenomenon and breaking it into small enough chunks so that it can be recapitulated or applied in some way. *Behavioral modeling* involves observing and mapping the successful processes which underlie an exceptional performance of some type. The purpose of behavior modeling is to create a pragmatic map or 'model' of a particular behavior which can be used to reproduce or simulate some aspect of that performance by anyone who is motivated to do so. The goal of the behavioral modeling process is to identify the essential elements of thought and action required to produce a particular desired response or outcome.

The field of Neuro-Linguistic Programming (NLP) has developed out of the modeling of the behaviors and thinking processes of exceptional people from many fields. NLP modeling procedures involve identifying the mental strategies ("Neuro") a person is using by analyzing that person's language patterns ("Linguistic") and non-verbal responses. The results of this analysis are then put into step-by-step strategies or procedures ("Programming") that may be used to transfer the skill to other people, and apply it to other contexts.

NLP has developed techniques and distinctions with which to identify and describe specific, reproducible patterns in the language and behavior of effective role models. The purpose of NLP modeling is to put what has been observed and described into action in a way that is productive and enriching. In fact, the worldwide success of NLP as a technology for creating and managing change comes from its foundation in the modeling process.

The second part of the book focuses on the application of NLP modeling procedures, illustrating their use in the study of effective leadership. It provides examples of how NLP was applied to identify specific cognitive, linguistic and behavioral skills used by leaders to address challenging situations involving problem solving, delegation and training on the job. The results define the key communication and relational skills employed by effective leaders to achieve practical results in their working reality.

Much of the material used as examples has been derived from a comprehensive study of leadership and creativity conducted for Fiat, in Turin, Italy, in the late 1980's and early 1990's. This work, combined with research into the processes of other effective leaders from all over the world, has also formed the basis for the companion volume to this book, *Visionary Leadership Skills* (1996), which presents the tools and skills necessary for "creating a world to which people want to belong."

Enjoy this generative journey into the skills that will help to create our future.

Chapter 1

Overview of Neuro-Linguistic Programming

Overview of Chapter 1

- **Neuro-Linguistic Programming**
- **Principles of NLP**

  The Map is Not the Territory
  Life and Mind are Systemic
  The Law of Requisite Variety

- **Deep Structure and Surface Structure**

- **The 'Epistemology' of NLP**

Neuro-Linguistic Programming

The process of modeling to be explored in this book is based upon the principles and distinctions of Neuro-Linguistic Programming (NLP). NLP is a behavioral science that provides:

1. **An Epistemology** – A system of knowledge and values

2. **A Methodology** – Processes and procedures for applying knowledge and values

3. **A Technology** – Tools to aid in the application of knowledge and values

NLP contains a set of principles and distinctions which are uniquely suited to analyze and identify crucial patterns of values, behavior and interrelationships so that they may be put into pragmatic and testable implementations. It is based on a set of fairly simple, formal linguistic, neurological and behavioral patterns and distinctions which are in some ways more fundamental and content free than any other existing model of human thinking and interaction. NLP provides a way to look past the behavioral content of what people do to the more invisible forces behind those behaviors; to the structures of thought that allow people to perform effectively. The name "Neuro-Linguistic Programming" implies the integration of three different scientific fields.

The *neuro* componant of Neuro-Linguistics is about the nervous system. A large part of NLP has to do with understanding and using principles and patterns of the nervous system. According to NLP, thinking, remembering, creating, vision-making, and all other cognitive processes, are a result of programs executed within the human nervous system. Human experience is a combination or synthesis of the information that we receive and process through our nervous system. Experientially this has to do with sensing the world – seeing, feeling, hearing, smelling, and tasting.

Neuro-Linguistic Programming also draws from the field of *linguistics*. In the NLP view, language is in some ways a product of the nervous system, but language also stimulates and shapes the activity within our nervous systems. Certainly, language is one of the primary ways a person has to activate or stimulate the nervous systems of other people. Thus, effective communication and interaction has to do with how we use language to instruct, to stimulate, and to verbalize concepts, goals and issues related to a particular task or situation.

This leaves the notion of *programming*. Neuro-Linguistic Programming is based upon the idea that the processes of human learning, memory, and creativity, are a function of programs – neurolinguistic programs that function more or less effectively to accomplish particular objectives or outcomes. The implication of this is that, as human beings, we interact with our world through our inner programming. We respond to problems and approach new ideas according to the kind of mental programs that we have established – and not all programs are equal. Some programs or strategies are more effective for accomplishing certain kinds of activities than others.

There are overlaps between NLP and other systems of psychology because NLP draws from the neurological, linguistic and cognitive sciences. It also draws from principles of computer programming and systems theory. Its purpose is to synthesize together a number of different kinds of scientific theories and models. One value of NLP is that it brings together different types of theories into a single structure.

Most of the techniques and tools of NLP have been derived through a process called "modeling." The primary approach of NLP has been to model effective behaviors and the cognitive processes behind them. The NLP modeling process involves finding out about how the brain ("Neuro") is operating by analyzing language patterns ("Linguistic") and non-verbal communication. The results of this analysis are then put into step-by-step strategies or programs ("Programming") that may be used to transfer the skill to other people and areas of application.

NLP was originally developed by John Grinder and Richard Bandler (Bandler & Grinder, 1975, 1976, 1979) by modeling the shared cognitive, linguistic and behavioral patterns of exceptional psychotherapists such as Fritz Perls (Gestalt therapy), Virginia Satir (family therapy) and Milton Erickson (hypnotherapy). While, at first glance, a model based on the interactive skills of effective therapists may not seem relevant to other areas, such as management, teaching or leadership, when one thinks of the understanding of human nature, perception and motives it requires to influence someone's behavior therapeutically, one realizes that there may be a number of areas of overlap between the skills of effective therapists and the skills of effective teachers, leaders and managers. Regardless of the degree of overlap, the same modeling principles used to extract the meaningful therapeutic behaviors of these exceptional therapists may be used to find the behavioral, psychological and linguistic patterns of exceptional leaders, teachers and managers.

In fact, NLP has already been extensively applied to the study of how the mental strategies, language patterns and value systems influence a variety of educational and management related activities including *communication skills* (Dilts, et al, 1980, McMaster & Grinder, 1981; Richardson & Margoulis, 1981; Laborde, 1982; Dilts, 1983; Yeager, 1985; Eicher, 1987, Smith & Hallbom, 1988), *sales skills* (Moine, 1981; Dilts, 1982, 1983; Bagley & Reese, 1987), *negotiation skills* (Dilts, 1980, 1983; Early, 1986, LeBeau, 1987), *organizational development and training* (Dilts, 1979, Maron, 1979, Gaster, 1988, Dilts 1993, 1994), the management of *creativity and innovation* (Dilts, Epstein & Dilts, 1991, Dilts &

Bonissone, 1993), *recruitment and selection* (Bailey, 1984); and *leadership* (Pile, 1988; Gaster, 1988; Dilts, 1996).

NLP has both analytical and interactive tools that vary according to the level of behavior or relationship being analyzed - "accessing cues," "rapport," "perceptual positioning," "logical levels," "meta model" patterns, "submodalities," "strategies," "meta program patterns", "sleight of mouth" patterns, "well-formedness conditions" for outcomes,   etc., will each 'slice the pie' into different chunks that are appropriate for different types of interactions.

The multi-level framework provided by NLP makes it possible to package abstract conceptual information regarding global and cultural patterns and trends into a form that may be connected to concrete organizational instruments, training seminars and individual actions and behaviors. With the tools and processes provided by Neuro-Linguistic Programming it is possible to build a pragmatic model of the psychological elements necessary for effective leadership, thinking, and behavior.

The belief system of NLP is that while, on the one hand, we all have physical differences, and differences in our backgrounds of experiences, we also share a lot of common features, and that at the process level, we could actually learn from, say, somebody like an Albert Einstein. He might have taken a lifetime of experience to develop the mental programs that he used to formulate the theory of relativity; but once that program is developed, we can understand and apply its structure without the need for the same lifetime of experience. As an analogy, the amount of time it takes for a computer programmer to initially develop a software program is much longer than it takes to transfer that program to another computer after it has already been written.

Thus, while NLP is about identifying and appreciating individual differences and individual styles of thinking, it also asserts that we can learn from other people's experiences because there are fundamental similarities between our nervous systems.   We can also be enriched by other people's programs.

Perhaps the most important aspect of NLP is its emphasis on practicality. NLP concepts and training programs emphasize interactive, experiential learning contexts so that the principles and procedures may be readily perceived and understood. Furthermore, since NLP processes are drawn from effective human models, their value and underlying structures are often intuitively recognized by people with little or no previous experience.

Training programs involving NLP have been implemented in many major corporations and organizations throughout the world including Fiat, IBM, American Express, The US Army, The State Railway of Italy, Apple Computer, Xerox, Merrill Lynch, Mercedes Benz, BMW, and many others.

Principles of NLP

NLP is based upon a set of fundamental presuppositions about people and about reality that have important implications for all areas of human endeavor.

The Map is Not the Territory

NLP operates from the assumption that the map is not the territory. As human beings, we can never know reality, in the sense that we have to experience reality through our senses and our senses are limited. A bee looking at this same page would perceive it very differently than we do because the whole sensory organization of the bee is different. We can only make maps of the reality around us through the information that we receive through our senses and the connection of that information to our own personal memories and other experiences. Therefore, we don't tend to respond to reality itself, but rather to our own maps of reality.

From this perspective, there is no one 'right' or 'correct' map of the world. We all have our own world view and that world view is based upon the sort of neurolinguistic maps that we have formed. It's these neurolinguistic maps that will determine how we interpret and how we react to the world around us and give meaning to our behaviors and our experiences, more so than reality itself. Thus, it is generally not external reality that limits us, constrains us, or empowers us, but rather it is our map of that reality. The basic idea of NLP is that if you can enrich or widen your map, you will perceive more choices available to you given the same reality. The primary function of NLP tools and techniques is to help to widen, enrich or add to our maps of the world. The basic presupposition of NLP is that the richer your map of the world is, the more possibilities that you have of dealing with whatever challenges occur in reality.

Life and 'Mind' are Systemic

A second presupposition of NLP is that life and mind are
systemic processes. That is, we are a system of interactions
made up of many sub-systems, and we are also a system within
a series of larger systems. The interactions that happen within
a human being, and between human beings and their environment, are systemic and occur according to certain systemic
principles. Our bodies, our interpersonal relationships and our
societies form a kind of ecology of systems and subsystems, all of
which are mutually influencing each other.

On one level, it's not possible to completely isolate any one
part of a system from another. People are influenced by
many aspects of the system around them. It is important to
take into account not only the processes that are happening
within the individual, but also the influences on that person
from the system around him or her. For instance, a person or
process that is effective in one type of system or environment
may be constrained or inhibited in another. We need to
consider the total system of interaction that is stimulating,
encouraging and influencing a particular phenomenon or
process.

The Law of Requisite Variety

In systems theory there is a principle called the 'Law of
Requisite Variety'. This principle is very important with
respect to effective performance of any type. The implication
of the Law of Requisite Variety is that we need to be
constantly exploring variations in the operations and the
processes that we use to get results. Even processes that
have been effective in the past might not continue to be
effective if the environment or the system around it changes.
In other words, one of the traps or limits to creativity is past
success. It's easy to believe that because something was
successful before, it will continue to be successful. But if

there are changes in the system around it, those things which used to work will no longer continue to function.

Specifically, the Law of Requisite Variety states that "in order to successfully adapt and survive, a member of a system needs a certain minimum amount of flexibility, and that flexibility has to be proportional to the potential variation or the uncertainty in the rest of the system." In other words, if someone is committed to accomplishing a certain goal, he or she needs to have a number of possible ways to reach it. The number of options required to be certain the goal can be reached depends on the amount of change that is possible within the system in which one is attempting to achieve the goal.

As a simple example, let's say someone has a goal to move a chair across a room. When there's not much variation in the environment, the person doesn't need much flexibility to accomplish that goal. He or she picks up the chair and carries it directly across the room. If that same person were in California, however, and there was an earthquake, he or she would have to have more potential variability to reach that goal because of changes being introduced in the environment. The person might even have to dodge a piece of the ceiling falling. Flexibility is needed to adapt and survive.

The point is that determining the amount of flexibility required by a situation is a result of assessing relationships of members of a system to the system itself. And, in fact, under times and contexts of change, flexibility becomes more essential.

Another implication of the Law of Requisite Variety is that the member of a system that has the most flexibility also tends to be the catalytic member of that system. This is a significant principle for leadership in particular. The ability to be flexible and sensitive to variation is important in terms of managing the system itself.

A key issue in effective performance is how to balance willingness to change with values such as 'consistence' and 'congruence' in behavior. The answer has to do with where we put the flexibility. If one is consistent with respect to his or her goal, one will have to have flexibility in how he or she reaches the goal. The issue has to do with at which levels we are flexible. In one sense, where you need to be flexible is determined by where you are determined to be inflexible. If somebody is determined to be competent at, say, leading or motivating people, then that is what they're holding constant. Where they need the flexibility is in being able to adapt to different motivations of people, and in being flexible when going into different environments.

As another example, let's say a musician wants to be consistent in producing a certain kind of sound with a certain kind of quality. This person has to be able to adapt to the acoustical variation of different concert halls, different musical instruments, etc. If somebody really is competent, they have to have flexibility in certain areas and inflexibility in others. So the notion of flexibility has to be viewed with respect to the total system. Competence involves consistency. But as soon as you are consistent in one area, you need to have flexibility in another area to be able to accommodate to the part of the system that is not changing.

As another concrete example, in California they have big skyscrapers that they want to remain very stable. But in order to make sure that the big skyscraper stays stable in an earthquake, they have to build a foundation that is able to tolerate movements of 16 feet side to side. One of the real secrets of managing creativity effectively is determining where to put the point of flexibility. It is ultimately a matter of ecology.

Deep Structure and Surface Structure

The NLP notions of "deep structure" and "surface structure" are derived from Noam Chomsky's theories of transformational grammar (1957, 1966). According to Chomsky, thoughts, concepts and ideas (deep structures) are not inherently related to any particular language, but may be expressed through a variety of linguistic expressions (surface structures). The English word "house," the French word "chez," and the Spanish word "casa," for example, refer to the same mental concept and experiential data. Similarly, the statements "The cat chased the rat," and "The rat was chased by the cat," both refer to the same event, even though the sequencing of the words is quite different. Complex thoughts and ideas reach the surface, as language, after a series of 'transformations' convert them into well-formed sentences and phrases. ("The the by was chased rat cat," uses the same words as "The rat was chased by the cat," but is not "well-formed.") These transformations act as a type of filter on our experiential deep structures.

According to Bandler and Grinder in *The Structure of Magic Volume I* (1975), the movement from deep structure to surface structure necessarily involves the processes of deletion, generalization and distortion:

The most pervasive paradox of the human condition which we see is that the processes which allow us to survive, grow, change, and experience joy are the same processes which allow us to maintain an impoverished model of the world - our ability to manipulate symbols, that is, to create models. So the processes which allow us to accomplish the most extraordinary and unique human activities are the same processes which block our further growth if we commit the error of mistaking the model of the world for reality. We can identify three general mechanisms by which we do this: Generalization, Deletion, and Distortion.

Generalization *is the process by which elements or pieces of a person's model become detached from their original experience and come to represent the entire category of which the experience is an example. Our ability to generalize is essential to coping with the world...The same process of generalization may lead a human being to establish a rule such as "Don't express any feelings."*

Deletion *is a process by which we selectively pay attention to certain dimensions of our experience and exclude others. Take, for example, the ability that people have to filter out or exclude all other sound in a room full of people talking in order to listen to one particular person's voice...Deletion reduces the world to proportions which we feel capable of handling. The reduction may be useful in some contexts and yet be the source of pain for us in others.*

Distortion *is the process which allows us to make shifts in our experience of sensory data. Fantasy, for example, allows us to prepare for experiences which we may have before they occur...It is the process which has made possible all the artistic creations which we as humans have produced...Similarly, all the great novels, all the revolutionary discoveries of the sciences involve the ability to distort and misrepresent present reality.*

Grinder and Bandler are suggesting that some information is necessarily lost or distorted in the transformation from deep structure to surface structure. In language, these processes occur during the translation of *deep structure* (the mental images, sounds, feelings and other sensory representations that are stored in our nervous systems) to *surface structure* (the words, signs and symbols we choose to describe or represent our primary sensory experience).

This is another way of saying that the models we make of the world around us with our brains and our language are not the world itself but representations of it. Many important clues about the deep structure, however, are expressed and reflected in the verbal surface structure.

The Meta Model was developed by Bandler and Grinder as a means to work with the surface structure of language in order to help a person to enrich their model of the world by recovering their deeper structure and reconnecting with their primary experience.

NLP has widened the use of the notions of 'deep structure' and 'surface structure' to include more than linguistic processes and representations. NLP considers deep structure to be composed of sensory and emotional experiences - or "primary experience." NLP views language as "secondary experience" – that is, a part of our model of the world that is derived from our primary experience.

Symbols, movements, songs, facial expressions, and other aspects of our behavior, however, are also forms of "surface structures" which we use to express our deeper structure (and are also subject to various forms of deletion, distortion and generalization).

Deep Structure

Ideas, Emotions, Values and Identity

Deletion
Distortion
Generalization

Physical , Verbal and Other Concrete Expressions

Movements   Words   Pictures

Surface Structures

Deep Structures Reach the Surface as a Result of a Series of Transformations Which Act as Filters on Our Primary Experience

As an example of the relationship between 'deep structure' and 'surface structures', most of us learned to write using our right or left hand. Yet, once we have learned this skill with our hand, it can be immediately transferred to other parts of the body. For instance, we can probably all write a reasonable facsimile of our names in the sand with our left big toe, or make letters by holding a pencil in our mouth (subject, or course, to a certain amount of distortion), even though the physical structure of these parts of our bodies are completely different. The deep structure related to the form of the letters is not tied to any particular part of the body. It can be generalized to many surface structures.

Thus, different surface structures may also be reflections of common deep structures.

Another important implication of the principles of transformational grammar is that there are multiple levels of successively deeper structures in the structure and organization of systems. An important consequence of this is that all levels of a system's structure should be addressed in order to achieve ecological change.

The NLP notion of Logical Levels (Dilts, 1990, 1991, 1993, 1995, 1996) is another way to organize the relationship between surface structure and deeper structures. Each of the levels (environment, behavior, capabilities, beliefs, values and identity) are considered to be successively deeper structures than the levels below them. Our perceptions and interactions with the environment are the part of our experience that is closest to the "surface." Coordinating and managing behavior requires the mobilization of deeper structures in our neurology. Our capabilities organize and coordinate our behaviors, involving less concrete but deeper processes. Beliefs and values are the underpinnings of our capabilities and behaviors. They are more difficult to express clearly and specifically at the surface, but they influence us at the deepest level. Identity is a very deep set of relationships that can best be described as a "function," analogous to the equations used to create a mathematical fractal.

Similar to Chomsky's ideas about language, the deep structure of our identity reaches the surface through a series of transformations which move through values, beliefs, capabilities and finally behavioral actions in the world. These transformations also are subject to deletion, generalization and distortion. These deletions, generalizations and distortions are the focus of the various techniques and models of NLP.

One of the goals of NLP is to identify problematic generalizations, deletions or distortions through the analysis of the 'syntax' or form of the surface structure and provide a system of tools so that a more enriched representation of the deep structure may be attained.

Another goal of NLP, represented by the modeling process, is to be able to create better links and pathways between surface structures and deep structures.

The 'Epistemology' of NLP

Epistemology is the discipline which systematically explores the structures and processes which underlie human knowledge. The term "epistemology" comes from the Greek words *epi* (meaning 'above' or 'upon'), *histanai* (meaning to 'set' or 'place') and *logos* (meaning 'word' or 'reason') - i.e., "that upon which we set our reasoning." An epistemology, then, is the fundamental system of distinctions and assumptions upon which one bases, and generates, all other knowledge. As Gregory Bateson defined it:

> *"Epistemology is the history of the origins of knowledge; in other words how you know what you know."*

The epistemology of NLP begins with the presupposition that 'the map is not the territory' – each of us actualizes possibilities in the world through the models or maps we create in our minds. NLP teaches that no one map is any more true or real than any other, but that your ability to be effective and evolve beyond where you are now is a function of having a map which permits the greatest possible range of choices. In NLP terms, then, a master is not someone who already knows the answers and has the solutions but someone who is able to ask worthwhile questions and direct the process of learning, problem solving and creativity to form new maps of the world that lead to useful new answers and possibilities.

The goal of mastering NLP is to learn how to model and apply the tools and principles of modeling to develop flexibility at the deepest levels of ourselves. Epistemology involves exploring the hidden presuppositions underlying different models of personal organization; the ones we share as well as the ones which make us unique.

The application of epistemology has to do with the system of distinctions and skills an individual or organization applies to meet espoused values and achieve goals. An applied epistemology must answer such questions as "How do we know that we know something or have operational competence?" "How do we know that others know something or have operational competence?" and "Through what means do we develop knowledge and operational competence?"

Applied epistemology also has to do with the system of values and goals promoted by a particular approach. For instance, the philosophy of NLP is that effective learning and change involves initially setting goals, evidence and evidence procedures to reach a particular desired state. A wide coverage of strategies and activities are then provided in order to be able to vary the operations applied to reach goals.

Another important question for applied epistemology is, "How does what you know, have learned, or discovered, fit in with what is already 'known'?" Until a new idea is harmonized with what is already known, it will not be put into practice – regardless of how 'brilliant' it is. One of the most important tasks of applied epistemology and modeling is to make it possible for people to understand ideas which challenge and transform old ways of thinking. This is especially challenging when those people are still thinking in the old way. According to the philosopher Arthur Schopenhauer, all great new ideas go through three stages. The first is ridicule; the second is violent opposition; then, finally, they are accepted as having always been 'self-evident'.

Molecular geneticist Gunther Stent (1987) maintains that much of the struggle related to the acceptance of new ideas and paradigms stems from a "contradictory epistemological attitude toward events in the outer and inner world." Stent identifies these conflicting philosophies as 'materialism' versus 'idealism' (or 'constructivism'). The materialist point of view essentially maintains that there is a 'real' external world that exists independently of the mind. The mind is a reflection of that reality and creates an imperfect representation of that real world. From the 'idealist' (or 'constructivist') perspective, reality is constructed by the mind. Perceived events and relations have no reality other than their existence in human thought. From this point of view, reality is a reflection of the mind. The external world is an imperfect representation or projection of 'pure' forms of thought. Stent points out that in recent years a third alternative has been emerging, spurred by Chomsky's theory of transformational grammar and the notion of surface structure and deep structure. He calls this new epistemology 'structuralism'. As Stent explains:

> *Both materialism and idealism take it for granted that all the information gathered by our senses actually reaches our mind; materialism envisions that thanks to this information reality is mirrored in the mind, whereas idealism envisions that thanks to this information reality is constructed by the mind. Structuralism, on the other hand, has provided the insight that knowledge about the world enters the mind not as raw data but in highly abstracted form, namely as structures. In the preconscious process of converting the primary data of our experience step by step into structures, information is necessarily lost, because the creation of structures, or the recognition of patterns, is nothing else than the selective destruction of information. Thus since the mind does not gain access to the full set of data about the world, it can neither mirror nor construct reality. Instead for the mind reality is a set of structural transforms of primary data taken from the world. This transformation process is hierarchical, in that "stronger" structures are formed from "weaker" structures through selective destruction of information. Any set of primary data becomes meaningful only after a series of such operations has*

*so transformed it that it has become congruent with a
stronger structure preexisting in the mind...canonical
knowledge is simply the set of preexisting "strong"
structures with which primary scientific data are
made congruent in the mental-abstraction process.
Hence data that cannot be transformed into a structure
congruent with canonical knowledge are a dead end.*

These fundamental epistemological distinctions can be
characterized as:

Materialism

There is a 'real' external world that exists independently of
the mind. The mind is a reflection of that reality and
creates an imperfect representation of that real world.

In Materialism, the Mind is Like a Camera that Takes Pictures of "Reality"

Idealism

Perceived events and relations have no reality other than
their existence in human thought. Reality is a reflection of
the mind. The external world is an imperfect representation or projection of 'pure' forms of thought.

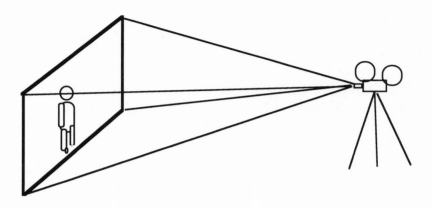

In Idealism, the Mind is Like a Projector that Creates "Reality"

Structuralism

Reality is a set of structural transforms of primary data taken from the world. The conversion of primary data into structures involves the selective deletion, distortion or generalization of primary data. The mind can neither mirror nor construct reality. "Stronger" structures are formed from "weaker" structures through selective destruction of information. Primary data becomes meaningful only after a series of such operations has transformed it to be congruent with a preexisting structure.

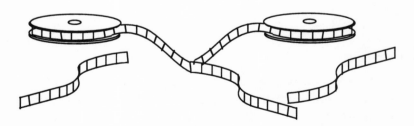

In Structuralism, the Mind is Like an Editor that Interacts with and Selects "Primary Data"

From the perspective of structuralism, many ideas are 'premature' if there is no bridge to existing 'canonical' knowledge. Thus, for a new idea to become "reality" it. must first 'pace' and then 'lead' the preexisting models of reality. Einstein's theory of relativity, for instance, encompassed and acknowledged all of Newton's laws, adding new formulations that have opened the door to new realities (such as atomic energy). Ideas that are too far ahead of their time must wait to become manifest. In order for Leonardo's flying machines or Tesla's robots to be brought into reality, they had to wait for the rest of the necessary knowledge to come into existence.

Stent points out that Gregor Mendel's studies of the inherited traits in sweet peas existed for 35 years before it was "rediscovered" by biologists at the end of the 19th century, becoming the cornerstone of modern genetics. Stent explains:

> *Mendel's discovery made no immediate impact, it can be argued, because the concept of discrete hereditary units could not be connected with canonical knowledge of anatomy and physiology in the middle of the 19th century. Furthermore, the statistical methodology by means of which Mendel interpreted the results of his pea-breeding experiments was entirely foreign to the way of thinking of contemporary biologists. By the end of the 19th century, however, chromosomes and the chromosome-dividing processes of mitosis and meiosis had been discovered and Mendel's results could now be accounted for in terms of structures visible in the microscope. Moreover, by then the application of statistics to biology had become commonplace.*

The epistemology of NLP is probably closest to that of structuralism, as opposed to either materialism or idealism. Unlike either materialism or idealism, the epistemology of

NLP is not based on a fundamental separation between "mind" and "reality." Similar to structuralism, NLP acknowledges the importance of creating links to existing knowledge, and expanding reality by pacing and leading. Rather than view the process of actualizing reality as being that of connecting "weaker" to "stronger" structures, however, NLP perceives it as a function of the connection between "deep" structure and "surface" structures. "Deep structures" are latent potentials that become manifest in concrete surface structures as a result of a set of transformations. This process includes the selective "construction" of data as well as the selective "destruction" of data (which Stent identifies as the primary process of pattern recognition in structuralism).

Building one's "dream house," for example, would involve a series of transformations, each one operating upon the previous transformation, allowing the dream to move from a fantasy to a completed building. Such a process may involve a sequence of "transformations" including:

Forming a mental picture of the house from various perspectives

Discussions with an architect

Preliminary drawings

Final plans

Selection of materials

Preparation of the building site

Laying the foundation

Framing the house

Completing construction

Painting the walls and woodwork

Doing the "finish" work

The degree to which the finished building matches one's initial dream is a function of the degree of generalization, deletion, distortion, and "addition," which occurs as a result of each successive transformation.

Different types and sequences of transformations would be required to convert a concept into an article or book, do a needs analysis of a group, express a feeling as a poem, identify a law of physics, write a computer program, memorize the lines of a play, etc.

From the NLP perspective, there are *inductive* transformations, through which we perceive patterns in, and build maps of, the world around us; and there are *deductive* transformations, through which we describe and act on our perceptions and models of the world. Inductive transformations involve the process of "chunking up" to find the deeper structure patterns ("concepts," "ideas," "universals," etc.) in the collections of experiences we receive through our senses. Deductive transformations operate to "chunk down" our experiential deep structures into surface structures; rendering general ideas and concepts into specific words, actions and other forms of behavioral output. (It involves a different set and sequence of transformations to learn to understand the vocabulary of a language, for example, than it does to learn to fluently speak a language in well-formed sentences and with the correct pronunciation – although some transformations may be applied during both processes.)

It is the development of both types of transformational processes that allow us to evolve our mental models, on the one hand, and express them in "reality," on the other. According to NLP, it is the quality of these transformations that determines the effectiveness and usefulness of our mental operations.

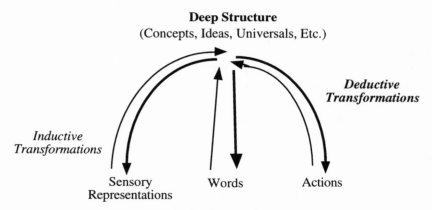

Deep Structure
(Concepts, Ideas, Universals, Etc.)

Deductive Transformations

Inductive Transformations

Sensory Representations   Words   Actions

Surface Structures

Environmental Input   *Behavior Outputs*

Mental Operations Connect Deep Structures to Surface Structures Through Inductive and Deductive Transformations

There are also what can be called *abductive* transformations, in which deep structures are transformed into other deep structures, and surface structures are transformed into other surface structures. This would involve processes such as metaphors and analogies. Analogies, such as "the sheep's fleece was as white as snow," or "her lips were like a red rose," are based on similes, which map between one surface structure and another ("isomorphism"). Metaphors, such as talking about "mother nature" or "spaceship earth," imply relationships between deeper structures ("homomorphism"). Such transformations are obviously at the basis of poetry and certain types of creative inspiration, but are also a fundamental process in problem solving and learning in general.

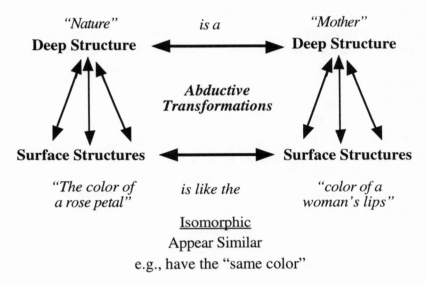

Homomorphic
Share Common
Fundamental Processes
e.g., are "Creative and Nurturing"

"Nature" — is a — *"Mother"*
Deep Structure ⟷ **Deep Structure**

Abductive
Transformations

Surface Structures ⟷ **Surface Structures**

"The color of — is like the — *"color of a*
a rose petal" — — *woman's lips"*

Isomorphic
Appear Similar
e.g., have the "same color"

Abductive Transformations Map Between One Deep Structure and Another, or Between One Surface Structure and Another

In the NLP view, then, "reality" is the relationship and interaction between deep structures and surface structures. Thus, there are many possible "realities." It is not as if there is "a map" and "a territory," there are many possible territories and maps, and the territory is continually changing, partially as a function of the way in which people's maps lead them to interact with that territory.

The aspects of deep structure which become manifest, are those for which enough missing links (deletions, generalizations, distortions) have been filled in that the potential which is latent at the level of deep structure is able to complete the series of transformations necessary to become manifest in some form of surface structure.

It is for these reasons that NLP emphasizes modeling and flexibility as the core of its epistemology. Models are not intended to either reflect or construct a single objective reality. Rather, their purpose is to simulate some aspect of a possible reality. In NLP, for instance, it is not important whether or not a model is "true," but rather that it is "useful." In fact, all models can be perceived as symbolic or metaphoric, as opposed to reflective of reality. Whether the description being used is metaphorical or literal, the usefulness of a model depends on the degree to which it allows us to move effectively to the next step in the sequence of transformations connecting deeper structures and surface structures. Instead of "constructing" reality, models establish a set of functions that serve as a tool or a bridge between deep structures and surface structures. It is this bridge that forms our "understanding" of reality and allows us to generate new experiences and expressions of reality.

Chapter 2

Basic Principles of Modeling

Overview of Chapter 2

- **What is Modeling?**
- **Overview of Modeling in NLP**
- **Modeling Deep Structure and Surface Structure**
- **Levels of Modeling**
- **Modeling Capabilities**
- **The T.O.T.E.: Minimum Requirements for Modeling Effective Skills and Behaviors**
- **Levels of Complexity of Skills and Capabilities**
- **Basic Elements of Modeling**

What is Modeling?

Webster's Dictionary defines a model as "a simplified description of a complex entity or process" – such as a "computer model" of the circulatory and respiratory systems. The term comes from the Latin root *modus*, which means "a manner of doing or being; a method, form, fashion, custom, way, or style." More specifically, the word "model" is derived from the Latin *modulus*, which essentially means a "small" version of the original mode. A "model" of an object, for example, is typically a miniature version or representation of that object. A "working model" (such as that of a machine) is something which can do on a small scale the work which the machine itself does, or is expected to do.

The notion of a "model" has also come to mean "a description or analogy used to help visualize something (as an atom) that cannot be directly observed." It can also be used to indicate "a system of postulates, data, and inferences presented as a formal description of an entity or state of affairs."

Thus, a miniature train, a map of the location of key train stations, or a train schedule, are all examples of different possible types of models of a railway system. Their purpose is to emulate some aspect of the actual railway system and provide useful information to better manage interactions with respect to that system. A miniature train set, for instance, may be used to assess the performance of a train under certain physical conditions; a map of key train stations can help to plan the most effective itinerary to reach a particular city; a train schedule may be used to determine the timing required for a particular journey. From this perspective, the fundamental value of any type of model is its *usefulness*.

Overview of Modeling in NLP

Behavior modeling involves observing and mapping the successful processes which underlie an exceptional performance of some type. It is the process of taking a complex event or series of events and breaking it into small enough chunks so that it can be recapitulated in some way. The purpose of behavior modeling is to create a pragmatic map or 'model' of that behavior which can be used to reproduce or simulate some aspect of that performance by anyone who is motivated to do so. The goal of the behavior modeling process is to identify the essential elements of thought and action required to produce the desired response or outcome. As opposed to providing purely correlative or statistical data, a 'model' of a particular behavior must provide a description of what is necessary to actually achieve a similar result.

The field of Neuro-Linguistic Programming has developed out of the modeling of human behaviors and thinking processes. NLP modeling procedures involve finding out about how the brain ("Neuro") is operating, by analyzing language patterns ("Linguistic") and non-verbal communication. The results of this analysis are then put into step-by-step strategies or programs ("Programming") that may be used to transfer the skill to other people and content areas.

In fact, NLP began when Richard Bandler and John Grinder modeled patterns of language and behavior from the works of Fritz Perls (the founder of Gestalt therapy), Virginia Satir (a founder of family therapy and systemic therapy) and Milton H. Erickson, M.D. (founder of the American Society of Clinical Hypnosis). The first 'techniques' of NLP were derived from key verbal and non-verbal patterns Grinder and Bandler observed in the behavior of these exceptional therapists. The implication of the title of their first book, *The Structure of Magic* (1975), was that what seemed magical and unexplainable often had a deeper structure that, when illuminated, could be understood, communicated and put into practice by people other than the few exceptional 'wizards' who had initially performed the 'magic'. NLP is the process by which the relevant pieces of these people's behavior was discovered and then organized into a working model.

NLP has developed techniques and distinctions with which to identify and describe patterns of people's verbal and non-verbal behavior - that is, key aspects of what people say and what they do. The basic objectives of NLP are to model special or exceptional abilities and help make them transferable to others. The purpose of this kind of modeling is to put what has been observed and described into action in a way that is productive and enriching.

The modeling tools of NLP allow us to identify specific, reproducible patterns in the language and behavior of effective role models. While most NLP analysis is done by actually watching and listening to the role model in action, much valuable information can be gleaned from written records as well.

The objective of the NLP modeling process is not to end up with the one 'right' or 'true' description of a particular person's thinking process, but rather to make an *instrumental map* that allows us to apply the strategies that we have modeled in some useful way. An 'instrumental map' is one that allows us to act more effectively - the 'accuracy' or 'reality' of the map is less important than its 'usefulness'. Thus, the instrumental application of the behaviors or cognitive strategies modeled from a particular individual or group of individuals involves putting them into structures that allow us to use them for some practical purpose. This purpose may be similar to or different from that for which the model initially used them.

For instance, some common applications of modeling include:

1. Understanding something better by developing more 'meta-cognition' about the processes which underlie it -

in order to be able to teach about it, for example, or use it as a type of "benchmarking."

2. Repeating or refining a performance (such as in a sport or a managerial situation) by specifying the steps followed by expert performers or during optimal examples of the activity. This is the essence of the 'business process reengineering' movement in organizations.

3. Achieving a specific result (such as effective spelling or the treatment of phobias or allergies). Rather than modeling a single individual, this is often accomplished by developing 'techniques' based on modeling a number of different successful examples or cases.

4. Extracting and/or formalizing a process in order to apply it to a different content or context. For example, an effective strategy for managing a sports team may be applied to managing a business, and vice versa. In a way the development of the 'scientific method' has come from this type of process, where strategies of observation and analysis that were developed for one area of study (such as physics) have been applied to other areas (such as biology).

5. Deriving an inspiration for something which is loosely based on the actual process of the model. Sir Arthur Conan Doyle's portrayal of Sherlock Holmes which was based on the diagnostic methods of his medical school professor Joseph Bell is a good example of this.

Modeling Deep Structure and Surface Structure

NLP draws many of its principles and distinctions from the field of transformational grammar (Chomsky 1957, 1965) as a means to create models of people's verbal behavior. One of the essential principles of transformational grammar is that tangible behaviors, expressions, and reactions are 'surface structures' which are the result of bringing 'deeper structures' into reality.

This is another way of saying that the models we make of the world around us with our brains and our language are not the world itself but representations of it. One important implication of the principles of transformational grammar is that there are multiple levels of successively deeper structures in the structure and organization within any coding system. An important implication of this, with respect to modeling, is that it may be necessary to explore various levels of deep structure, behind a particular performance, in order to produce an effective model of it. Furthermore, different surface structures may be reflections of common deep structures. For effective modeling, it is frequently important to examine multiple examples of surface structures in order to better know or identify the deeper structure which produces it.

Another way to think about the relationship between deep structure and surface structure is the distinction between "process" and "product." Products are the surface level expressions of the deeper and less tangible generative processes which are their source. Thus, "deep structures" are latent potentials that become manifest in concrete surface structures as a result of a set of transformations. This process includes the selective destruction as well as the selective construction of data.

In this regard, one of the fundamental challenges of modeling comes from the fact that the movement between deep structure and surface structure is subject to the processes of generalization, deletion and distortion. That is, some information is necessarily lost or distorted in the transformation from deep structure to surface structure. In language, for example, these processes occur during the translation of deep structure (the mental images, sounds, feelings and other sensory representations that are stored in our nervous systems) to surface structure (the words, signs and symbols we choose to describe or represent our primary sensory experience). No verbal description is able to completely or acccurately represent the idea it is attempting to express.

The aspects of deep structure which become manifest, are those for which enough missing links (deletions, generalizations, distortions) have been filled in that the latent potential at the level of deep structure is able to complete the series of transformations necessary to become manifest as surface structure. One of the goals of the modeling process is to identify a complete enough set of transformations so that an appropriate and useful expression of the deep structure may be attained.

Levels of Modeling

Creating an effective model of a particular behavior or performance involves more than imitation. Depending on one's purpose for modeling, there may be several different levels of information required in order to achieve the desired performance or application. In modeling an individual, for example, there are a number of different aspects, or levels, of the various systems and sub-systems in which that person operates that we may explore.

At one level, for instance, one can look at the social and geographical *environment* influences on a person – i.e., *when* and *where* the person is acting or performing. That is, one can consider the external context; such as the state of marketplace, natural surroundings, work place, etc. Furthermore, one can examine both macro environments and micro environments. Micro environments would involve specific locations such as an individual's office, a particular building, classroom or factory, etc. Macro environments would include general habitat, social contexts, public events, etc. In addition to the influence these environments may have on the individual to be modeled, one can examine the influence and impact that the individual has or may have on the environment.

At another level, one can examine the specific *behaviors* and actions that a person engages in while performing – i.e., *what* specifically the person does within the environment. What are the particular patterns of work, interaction or communication related to collaborators, problems or goals? As with the environmental level, one can focus on either micro or macro behavioral patterns. Macro behaviors would involve general patterns of communication, work, style, etc. Micro behavioral patterns would involve more detailed and specific actions such as particular behaviors during tasks, specific work routines, work habits, etc.

One may also look at the intellectual and cognitive strategies and *capabilities* which are required for the actions within the identified environment – i.e., *how* a person generates the behaviors in that context. On a macro level, capabilities would include general strategies and skills such as learning, memory, motivation, decision making and creativity. On a micro level, examining a person's mental capabilities would involve detailing how the person used micro cognitive patterns such as visualization, internal dialog or self talk and his or her senses in the performance of a particular behavior or task.

One could further explore the *beliefs and values* that motivate and shape the thinking strategies and capabilities that are required to accomplish the behavioral goals in the environment – i.e., *why* a person does things in a particular time and place. On a macro level, basic beliefs relate to the type of meaning, cause-effect relations and boundaries people place on events or perceive in the surrounding world. On a micro level, a person's beliefs and values can relate to processes on other levels. That is, a person may have beliefs *about* his or her environment, behavior, capabilities, identity, work system, profession, community, etc. A person can even have beliefs about his or her beliefs, judging them as "good," "bad," "progressive," "in conflict," etc.

One could look even more deeply to investigate the perception of role or *identity* a person has in relation to his or her beliefs, capabilities and actions within a particuar environment – i.e., the *who* behind the why, how, what, where and when. This would involve potential issues relating to role definition, character traits, personality, etc. A key element in establishing a particular role or identity involves defining the sense of mission a person has within the larger system in which he or she is operating.

One might also want to examine the way in which a particular person operates within the relational context of family, colleagues, social class or culture – i.e., who the person is or will be in relation to *who and what else.* In other words, what is the *vision* of the individual with respect to the purpose of their behaviors, abilities, beliefs, values and identity within the larger systems of which he or she is a part? It is often this vision which gives all of the other levels their ultimate meaning.

One way to visualize the relationships between these elements is as a network of generative systems that focus or converge on the identity of the individual as the core of the modeling process.

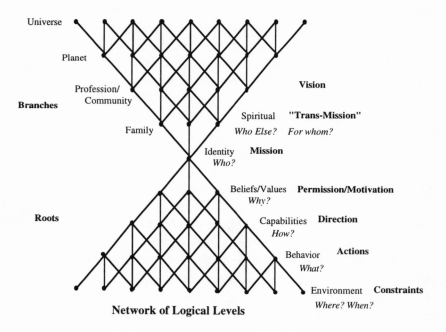

Network of Logical Levels

In summary, modeling may involve exploring the interactions of a number of different levels of experience, including:

Spiritual   Vision & Purpose
A. *Who I Am* –   Identity   Mission
B. *My Belief System* – Values, Expectations Permission
                                                  & Motivation
C. *My Capabilities* – States, Strategies   Direction
D. *What I Do* –   Specific Behaviors   Actions
E. *My Environment* – External Context   Reactions

- Environment determines the external opportunities or constraints to which a person must react. It involves the *where* and *when* of a particular skill or ability.

- Behaviors are the specific actions or reactions made by a person within the environment. It involves the *what* of a particular skill or ability.

- Capabilities guide and give direction to behavioral actions through a mental map, plan or strategy. It involves the *how* of a particular skill or ability.

- Beliefs and values provide the reinforcement (motivation and permission) that supports or inhibits capabilities. It involves the *why* of a particular skill or ability.

- Identity relates to a person's role, mission and/or sense of self. It involves the *who* of a particular skill or ability.

- Spiritual relates to the larger system of which one is a part. It involves the *who else* or *for whom* of a particular skill or ability.

Modeling Capabilities

The focus of most NLP modeling processes is at the level of capabilities, the *how to* level. Capabilities connect beliefs and values to specific behaviors. Without the *how*, knowing what one is supposed to do, and even why to do it, is largely ineffective. Capabilities and skills provide the links and leverage to manifest our vision, identity, values and beliefs as actions in a particular environment.

The fact that NLP modeling procedures tend to focus on capabilities, by the way, does not mean they only consider that level of information. Often, an entire gestalt of beliefs, values, sense of self, and specific behaviors are essential to produce the desired capability. NLP maintains that, by focusing on developing capabilities, the most practical and useful combinations of "deep structure" and "surface structure" will be produced.

It is important to keep in mind that capabilities are a deeper structure than specific tasks or procedures. Procedures are typically a sequence of actions or steps that lead to the accomplishment of a particular task. Skills and capabilities, however, are frequently "non-linear" in their application. A particular skill or capability (such as the ability to 'think creatively', or to 'communicate effectively') may serve as a support for many different kinds of tasks, situations and contexts. Capabilities must be able to be "randomly accessed," in that the individual must be able to immediately call upon different skills at different times in a particular task, situation or context. Instead of a linear sequence of steps, skills are thus organized around a T.O.T.E. – a feedback loop between (a) goals (b) the choice of means used to accomplish those goals and (c) the evidence used to assess progress towards the goals.

The T.O.T.E.: Minimum Requirements For Modeling Effective Skills and Behaviors

"The pursuance of future ends and the choice of means for their attainment are the mark and criterion of the presence of mentality in a phenomenon"

William James - ***Principles of Psychology***

The essential modeling framework employed by NLP is that of the goal oriented feedback loop described by the T.O.T.E. (Miller, Gallanter and Pribram, 1960). The letters T.O.T.E. stand for Test-Operate-Test-Exit. The T.O.T.E. concept maintains that all mental and behavioral programs revolve around having a fixed goal and a variable means to achieve that goal.

This model indicates that, as we think, we set goals in our mind (consciously or unconsciously) and develop a TEST for when that goal has been achieved. If that goal is not achieved we OPERATE to change something or do something to get closer to our goal. When our TEST criteria have been satisfied we then EXIT on to the next step. So the function of any particular part of a behavioral program could be to (T)est information from the senses in order to check progress towards the goal or to (O)perate to change some part of the ongoing experience so that it can satisfy the (T)est and (E)xit on to the next part of the program.

A TEST for effective "leadership," for example, might be that a particular project is 'profitable'. If the project is not profitable enough, the leader will need to OPERATE or go through procedures to attempt to make the project more profitable, or to come up with a more appropriate project.

Often, there are different ways to TEST for something like "profitability" based on different maps and assumptions about what it means to be 'profitable'. For instance, 'profitability' may be determined on the basis of:

a) physical possession of cash or other assets

b) comparisons made to other projects

c) what is seen as being the longer term benefits of the project

d) additional opportunities generated as the result of the project

These variations in evidences may make a significant difference in the kind of results produced by the project and in the people who are likely to be attracted to it. It is these types of sometimes subtle differences in tests and operations that can make the difference between an effective and ineffective performative.

Thus, according to NLP, in order to effectively model a particular skill or performance we must identify each of the key elements of the T.O.T.E. related to that skill or performance:

1. The performer's goals.

2. The evidence and evidence procedures used by the performer(s) to determine progress toward the goal.

3. The sets of choices used by the performer(s) to get to the goal and the specific behaviors used to implement these choices.

4. The way the performer(s) respond(s) if the goal is not initially achieved.

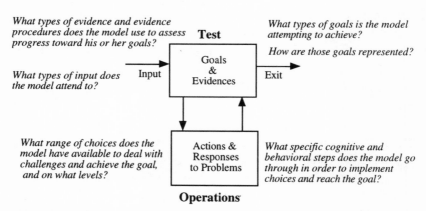

What types of evidence and evidence procedures does the model use to assess progress toward his or her goals?

Test

What types of goals is the model attempting to achieve?

How are those goals represented?

What types of input does the model attend to? Input | Goals & Evidences | Exit

What range of choices does the model have available to deal with challenges and achieve the goal, and on what levels?

Actions & Responses to Problems

What specific cognitive and behavioral steps does the model go through in order to implement choices and reach the goal?

Operations

Modeling Involves Defining the Various Elements of the Performer's T.O.T.E.

Levels of Complexity of Skills and Capabilities

It should be kept in mind that capabilities themselves are of different natures and levels of complexity. In attempting to model the goals, evidences, operations and responses to problems (the T.O.T.E. elements) employed by exceptional people, it is important to consider at which levels they may be directed. A 'goal', for example, may be stated in terms of specific behaviors, such as "produce twenty units by Friday." It may also be defined in terms of a capability, such as "improve our problem solving ability." A goal at the level of beliefs and values would be something like, "increase our focus on 'quality'." An identity level goal might be something like to "be the 'frontrunner' in our field." A goal defined in terms of a 'vision' would be something like "transform the way people communicate with another."

Obviously, these different levels of goals would also require different levels of evidences and operations, and would encounter different levels of problems. In fact, having the wisdom and skill to be able to manage the interrelations between these different levels of processes is probably one of the greatest challenges of effective performance of any type.

Some skills and capabilities are, in fact, made up of other skills and capabilities. The ability to "write a book" is made up the abilites relating to the vocabulary, grammar, and spelling of the language in which one is writing, as well as knowledge relating to the subject one is writing the book about. These are often referred to as "nested T.O.T.E.s," "sub-loops," or "sub-skills," because they relate to the smaller chunks out of which more sophisticated or complex skills are built. The capability of "leadership," for example, is made up of many sub-skills, such as those relating to effective communication, establishing rapport, problem solving, systemic thinking, and so on.

Thus, the modeling process itself may be directed toward different levels of complexity with respect to particular skills and capabilities.

1. *Simple Behavioral* skills would involve specific, concrete, easily observable actions that take place within short periods of time (seconds to minutes). Examples of simple behavioral skills would include: making a particular dance movement, getting into a special state, shooting a basket, aiming a rifle, etc.

2. *Simple Cognitive* skills would be specific, easily identifyable and testable mental processes which occur within a short period of time (seconds to minutes). Examples of simple cognitive skills would be: remembering names, spelling, acquiring simple vocabulary, creating a mental image, etc. These types of thinking skills produce easily observable behavioral results that can be measured, and provide immediate feedback.

3. *Simple Linguistic* skills would involve the recognition and use of specific key words, phrases and questions, such as: asking specific questions, recognizing and responding to key words, reviewing or 'backtracking' key phrases, etc. Again, the performance of these skills is easily observable and measurable.

4. *Complex Behavioral* (or Interactive) skills involve the construction and coordination of sequences or combinations of simple behavioral actions. Abilities such as juggling, learning a martial arts technique, successfully executing a play in a particular sport, making a presentation, acting a part in a film or play, etc., would be examples of complex behavioral skills.

5. *Complex Cognitive* skills are those which require a synthesis or sequence of other simple thinking skills. Creating a story, diagnosing a problem, solving an algebra problem, composing a song, planning a modeling project, etc., would be examples of capabilities involving complex cognitive skills.

6. *Complex Linguistic* skills would involve the interactive use of language in highly dynamic (an often spontaneous) situations. Abilities such as persuasion, negotiation, verbal reframing, using humor, storytelling, doing a hypnotic induction, etc., would be examples of capabilities involving complex linguistic skills.

Clearly, each level of skill needs to include and incorporate the abilities, or T.O.T.E.s, employed by the levels preceding it. Thus, it is typically more challenging and involved to model complex skills than simple ones; and it is easier to learn modeling by beginning with simple behavioral and cognitive skills before moving to more complex tasks. Often, however, complex skills can be "chunked down" into a group or sequence of simpler ones.

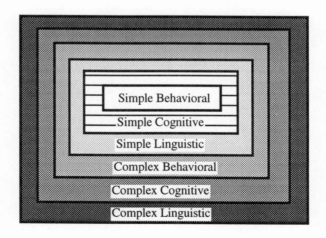

Skills Form Various Levels of Complexity

One key consideration in modeling, then, is determining at which level, or "chunk size," of skill one will be focusing. The distinctions and procedures which are successful for modeling one level of skill may not be as effective in modeling another level. For example, simple imitation, or "mirroring" may be a successful strategy for modeling simple behavioral skills, but be an ineffective means to model complex cognitive or linguistic skills. Likewise, a simple questionnaire or verbal interview may be enough to model a simple cognitive skill, but be inadequate to create an effective model for a complex, or even simple, behavioral skill.

Chapter 3

Modeling Methodology

Overview of Chapter 3

- **Modeling Methodology**
- **Three Basic Perspectives in Modeling**
- **Implicit and Explicit Modeling**
- **Basic Phases of Modeling**
- **Summary of the Steps in the Modeling Process**
- **Some Beginning Modeling Drills and Exercises**
- **Finding Relevant Patterns**
  Feature Detection
  Pattern Recognition
  Mill's Methods
- **Defining a Modeling Project**
- **Goals for the Modeling Process**

Modeling Methodology

One of the pivotal parts of the modeling process is the methodology used to gather information and identify relevant features and patterns relating to the T.O.T.E.s of the person(s) being modeled. This is known as *elicitation* in NLP. While standard forms of information gathering, such as questionnaires and interviews, can access some information, they often fall short of identifying the unconscious or intuitive operations used by a human expert. They also often assume or delete important information regarding context.

In addition to questionnaires and interviews, it is often useful and necessary to incorporate more active methods for gathering information such as role plays, simulations, and the 'real life' observation of the expert in context. While NLP modeling methodology does employ interviews and questionnaires, the primary form of modeling in NLP is done by interactively engaging the individual(s) to be modeled in multiple examples of the skill or performance to be studied. This provides the "highest quality" information, and creates the best chance to "capture" the most practical patterns (in the same way that having a living model is generally much more desirable for an artist to work from than a verbal description).

The most commonly used NLP elicitation methods involve either (1) recalling and reliving a specific experience, or (2) carrying out a task which presupposes or triggers a particular capability, strategy, resource or problem state. If a person is an excellent public speaker, for example, the person could be (a) asked to "think of a time when" he or she was giving a speech, or (b) asked to stand up in front of a group and talk. Similarly, to elicit a person's creative process, the person could be asked to (a) recall and relive a time when he or she was particularly creative, or (b) to do something creative on the spot, or in the moment.

The first method, of engaging memory, has advantages in that the individual can more easily get distance from the experience in order to 'think about' or 'reflect on' the structure of the experience. Additionally, if aspects of the experience are unpleasant, it can be easier for the person to dissociate from, or 'get out of' the experience. The disadvantages are that the person may give contaminated or mixed signals, because the person is continually having to go through the process of recall. He or she may move in and out of the state or experience being accessed, creating confusion for an inexperienced observer. Also, people tend to do a significant amount of filtering (deletion, distortion and generalization) as they are determining what to access and present to others.

The advantage of the second method is that it provides more immediate, 'higher quality' information about the experiences or states to be explored and utilized. There is less conscious filtering of the experience, and therefore more spontaneous, unconscious cues available. A disadvantage of this approach is that people can become 'caught in the content' of the experience, and be unable to easily reflect on their process or develop enough 'metacognition'. Alternatively, a problem can arise if people become overly self-conscious during the task or performance, causing them to become either uncomfortable or disassociated from their experience.

Another common and powerful form of elicitation is "acting as if." The process of acting 'as if' allows people to drop their current perception of the constraints of reality and use their imagination more fully. It utilizes people's innate ability to imagine and pretend in order to draw out or create responses. Acting 'as if' is one of the most profound ways of eliciting resources. When a person is stuck or confused, for instance, he or she may be asked to "act 'as if' you are confident and clear." This often helps people to access latent potentials that they have not been using.

Three Basic Perspectives in Modeling

Modeling often requires that we make a "double" or "triple" description of the process or phenomenon we are attempting to recreate. NLP describes three fundamental perceptual positions from which information can be gathered and interpreted: first position (associated in one's own perspective), second position (perceiving the situation from the standpoint of another person), and third position (viewing the situation as an uninvolved observer). All three of these perspectives are essential for effective behavioral modeling.

<ins>1st Position</ins>	<ins>2nd Position</ins>	<ins>3rd Position</ins>
Own Point of View	Other's Point of View	Outside Observer

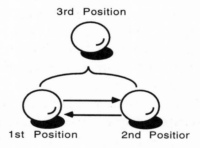

**Effective Modeling Involves Exploring a Particular
Phenomenon or Performance from Multiple Perspectives**

There is also a fourth perceptual position, which involves perceiving a situation from the perspective of the whole system, or the "relational field," involved in the situation.

Because NLP presupposes that "the map is not the territory," that "everyone forms their own individual map of a situation," and that there is no single "right" map of any particular experience or event, taking multiple perspectives is an essential skill in order to effectively model a particular performance or activity. Perceiving a situation or experience from multiple perspectives allows a person to gain broader insight and understanding with respect to the event.

Modeling from 'first position' would involve trying something out for ourselves, and exploring the way that "we" do it. We see, hear, and feel from our own perspective. 'Second position' modeling involves standing "in the shoes" of the person to be modeled, attempting to think and act as much like the other person as possible. This can provide important intuitions about significant but unconscious aspects of the thoughts and actions of the person being modeled. Modeling from 'third position' would involve standing back and observing the person to be modeled interacting with other people (including ourselves) as an uninvolved witness. In third position, we suspend our personal judgments and notice only what our senses perceive, as a scientist might objectively examine a particular phenomenon through a telescope or microscope. 'Fourth position' would involve a type of intuitive synthesis of all of these perspectives, in order to get a sense for the entire 'gestalt'.

Implicit and Explicit Modeling

Skilled performance can be described as a function of two fundamental dimensions: *consciousness* (knowing) and *competence* (doing). It is possible to know or understand some activity, but be unable to do it (conscious incompetence). It is also possible to be able to do a particular activity well, but not know how one does it (unconscious competence). Mastery of a skill involves both the ability to "do what you know," and to "know what you are doing."

One of the biggest challenges in modeling human experts comes from the fact that many of the critical behavioral and psychological elements which allow them to excel are largely unconscious and intuitive to them. As a result, they are unable to provide a direct description of the processes responsible for their own exceptional capabilities. In fact, many experts purposefully avoid thinking about what they are doing, and how they are doing it, for fear that it will actually interfere with their intuitions. This is another reason it is important to be able to model from different perceptual positions.

One of the goals of modeling is to draw out and identify people's *unconscious competences* and bring them to awareness in order to better understand, enhance and transfer them. For example, an individual's unconscious strategy, or T.O.T.E., for "knowing which questions to ask," "coming up with creative suggestions," or "adapting the non-verbal aspects of one's leadership style," can be modeled, and then transferred as a conscious skill or competence.

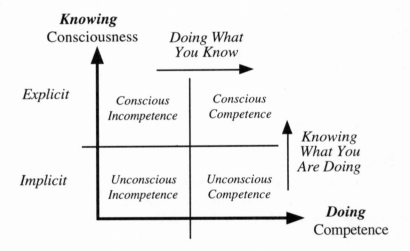

One of the Purposes of Modeling is to Help People to 'Do What They Know' and to 'Know What They Are Doing'

Cognitive and behavioral competences may be modeled either 'implicitly' or 'explicitly'. *Implicit modeling* involves primarily moving to 'second position' with the modeling subject in order to build personal intuitions about that individual's subjective experience. *Explicit modeling* involves moving to a 'third position' to describe the explicit structure of the modeling subject's experience so that it may be transferred to others. The table below lists some of the key differences between the two types of modeling processes:

Implicit:	**Explicit:**
Experience—>Intuition—>Self Use (Build Subjective Experience from *Second Position*)	Intuition—>Structure—>Transfer to Others (Define the Structure of Subjective Experience from *Third Position*)

IMPLICIT	**EXPLICIT**
Unconscious	Conscious
"Right Brain"	"Left Brain"
General - Whole	Specific - Parts
Synthetic	Sequential
State	Strategy
Associated	Disassociated
Inductive	Deductive
Intuitive	Cognitive
Analog	Digital
Child	Adult
External—>Internal	Internal—>External
Territory	Map

Comparison of Implicit and Explicit Modeling

Implicit modeling is primarily an inductive process by which we take in and perceive patterns in the world around us. Explicit modeling is essentially a deductive process by which we describe and put those perceptions into practice. Both processes are necessary for effective modeling. Without the "implicit" phase, there is no effective intuition base from which to build an "explicit" model. As NLP co-founder John Grinder pointed out, "It is impossible to make a description

of the grammar of a language about which you have no
intuition." On the other hand, without the "explicit" phase,
the information that has been modeled cannot be built into
techniques or tools and transferred to others.   Implicit
modeling by itself will help a person to develop personal,
unconscious competence with the desired behavior (the way
that young children typically learn). Creating a technique,
procedure or skill set that can be taught or transferred to others
beyond oneself, however, requires some degree of explicit modeling. It is one thing, for example, to learn to spell well, or develop
an effective golf swing for oneself; it is another thing to teach
other people how to do what you have learned.

NLP, in fact, was born from the union of implicit and
explicit modeling. Richard Bandler had been intuitively
"implicitly" modeling the linguistic skills of Fritz Perls and
Virginia Satir through video tapes and direct experience.
Bandler was able to reproduce many of the therapeutic
results of Perls and Satir by asking questions and using
language in a similar manner as they did. Grinder, who was
a linguist, observed Bandler working one day, and was
impressed by Bandler's ability to influence others with his
use of language. Grinder could sense that Bandler was doing
something systematic, but was unable to explicitly define
what it was. Bandler was also unable to explicitly describe
or explain exactly what he was doing and how he was doing
it. He only knew that he had somehow "modeled" it from
Perls and Satir. Both men were intrigued and curious to
have a more explicit understanding of these abilities that
Bandler had implicitly modeled from these exceptional therapists - an understanding that would allow them to transfer it
as a 'conscious competence' to others. At this point Grinder
made the offer to Bandler, "If you teach me to do what you
are doing, then I will tell you what you are doing."

In a very real way, Grinder's historic invitation marks the
beginning of NLP. Grinder's words encapsulate the essence
of the NLP modeling process: "If you teach me to do what

you are doing" (if you help me to develop the implicit intuitions, or 'unconscious competence', that you possess so that I too can accomplish similar results), "then I will tell you what you are doing" (then I can make an explicit description of the patterns and processes we are both using). Notice that Grinder did *not* say, "If you let me objectively observe and statistically analyze what you are doing, then I will tell you what you are doing." Grinder said, "Teach *me* to *do* what you are doing." Modeling arises from the practical and instrumental intuitions that come from "leading with experience."

Grinder and Bandler were able to work together to create the Meta Model (1975) by synthesizing (a) their shared intuitions about the verbal capabilities of Perls and Satir, (b) direct observations (either in life or through video tape) of Perls and Satir as they worked, and (c) Grinder's explicit knowledge of linguistics (in particular, transformational grammar).

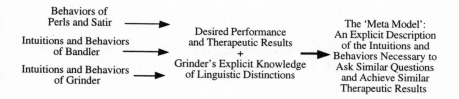

The Meta Model Arose from the Combination of Bandler and Grinder's Intuitions, the Observable Behavior of Perls and Satir, and Grinder's Explicit Knowledge of Linguistics

Bandler and Grinder next collaborated to apply a similar process in order to model some of the Hypnotic language patterns of Milton H. Erickson; this time with Grinder also participating in the initial "implicit" modeling of Erickson's behavior. They, and other NLP developers, have since used this process of modeling to create innumerable strategies, techniques and procedures in practically every area of human competence.

The Basic Phases of Modeling

The basic phases of the typical NLP modeling process reflect the movement from implicit to explicit modeling encapsulated by Grinder's initial proposition to Bandler. These phases include:

Preparation

Preparation for modeling involves selecting a person who has the capability you wish to model, and determining:

a) the context in which you will do the modeling
b) where and when you will have access to the person to be modeled
c) what relationship you want with the person to be modeled
d) what state you will be in while doing the modeling

It also includes establishing the appropriate conditions, anchors, and 'life lines', that will allow you to fully commit to the project.

Phase 1- Unconscious Uptake

The first phase of the modeling process involves engaging the person to be modeled in an example of the desired performance or capability within the appropriate context. You begin "modeling" by going to 'second position' in order to build intuitions about the skills that the person is demonstrating. This is done without observing for any specific patterns. Instead, simply take on the posture and physiology of the model and attempt to identify yourself with him or her internally. It is sometimes best to take on the micro muscle movements of the individual rather than mirror the obvious actions of the person. The overt behavior of the model is the 'surface structure'. Micro muscle movements and second position shifts will enable you to get to more of the deep structure behind it. (Also, sometimes overt mirroring can be distracting to the individual you are modeling.)

This is the phase of "unconscious uptake." Do not try to consciously understand what the model is doing (yet). Setting up filters may cause you to lose important information. You do not yet know what is important and what is not. At this phase, it is often useful to begin from a state of "not knowing." This is a state in which all previous mental maps and assumptions are put aside with reference to one's ongoing experience. (This is sometimes humorously referred to as a "Nerk-Nerk" state, named after a fictitious space alien invented by NLP trainer and developer Todd Epstein. "Nerk-Nerk" can see, hear and feel everything that we can, but does not have any of our assumptions or interpretations about what he is experiencing.) When a person enters a state of "not knowing," he or she attempts to drop any pre-existing assumptions, and to get a fresh and unbiased view of a particular situation or experience.

Once you feel that you have developed a good set of intuitions from being in 'second position' with the person you are modeling, arrange for a context where you can use the skill that you have been exploring. Begin to try out the skill within that context "as if" you were the person you have been modeling. Then, attempt to achieve the same result just being "yourself." This will give you what is known as a "double description" of the particular skill you are modeling. When the responses you get are roughly the same as those that the model gets, then the first phase of modeling is complete.

Phase 2 - The Subtraction Process

The next step in the modeling process is to sort out what is essential in the model's behavior from what is extraneous. (A person does not need to sit in a wheelchair and wear purple pajamas, like Milton Erickson did, for example, in order to be able achieve similar therapeutic results using hypnosis.) At this stage, you start to be explicit about the strategies and behaviors you have modeled. Since you are able to get similar responses to the person you have modeled, you will want to use your own 'first position' behavior as a reference as well. (That is, enacting the skill "as yourself" rather than "as if" you were the individual you have been modeling.)

Your objective is to clarify and define the specific cognitive and behavioral steps that are required to produce the desired results in the chosen context(s). At this stage, you will also want to begin to systematically leave out pieces of any of the behaviors or strategies you have identified, in order to see what makes a difference. Anything you leave out that makes no difference to the responses you get is not essential to the model. When you leave out something that makes a difference to the results you get, you have identified a crucial part of the model. This is called the "subtraction process." Its purpose is to reduce the steps you have modeled to their simplest and most elegant form, and separate the essential from "superstition."

When you have completed this stage, you will have your current 'minimum model' of how you replicate the model's capabilities in yourself (i.e., from your 'first position'). You will also have your 'second position' intuitions of the model's capabilities that you have developed from placing yourself in his or her "shoes." In addition, you will have a 'third position', perspective from which you can notice the difference between the way you replicate the model's capability and how that person manifested the capability in his or her original way. This is known in NLP as a "triple description."

Phase 3 - Design

The final phase of modeling involves designing a context and procedure which enables others to learn the skills you have modeled, and thus be able to get the results that the person who served as the model has been able to achieve. To produce the design, you will want to synthesize the information that you have gained from all three perceptual positions. Rather than simply mimic or imitate the specific steps followed by the person you have modeled, for instance, it is generally most effective to create the appropriate reference experiences for the learners that will help them to discover and develop the particular "circuits" that they will need to perform the skill effectively. It is not necessary to force them to go through the same modeling process that you went through to gain the skill.

Different students will have differing conscious and unconscious competences as their "starting states." This is important to factor into your design. If a particular procedure that you have modeled requires visualization, for instance, some students may already be able to do this quite effectively, while for others, it may be a completely novel idea. Thus, some students may be able to combine multiple steps in the procedure together into a single step, while others will have to break a particular step into smaller sub-skills.

Again, the guiding principle is the "usefulness" of your design for the students for which the model is intended.

Summary of the Steps in the Modeling Process

We can summarize the basic phases of the NLP modeling process in the following sequence of steps:

1. Determine the human experts to be modeled, and the contexts in which they apply the capability to be modeled.

2. Set up and carry out the appropriate information gathering procedure in the appropriate contexts, from different perceptual positions. Start by building intuitions from 'second position', then try to reproduce the results from your own 'first position'. Take a 'third position' and notice any differences between your way, and that of the person you have modeled.

3. Filter the results of the information gathering procedure for relevant cognitive and behavioral patterns.

4. Organize the patterns into a logical, coherent structure or "model."

5. Test the effectiveness/usefulness of the model you have constructed by trying them out in various contexts and situations, and making sure you are able to achieve the desired results.

6. Reduce the model to the simplest and most elegant form that will still produce the desired results.

7. Identify the best procedures to transfer, or "install," the explicit skills identified by the modeling process.

8. Determine the most appropriate instruments to measure the results of the model, and find the limits or the 'edge' of the model's validity.

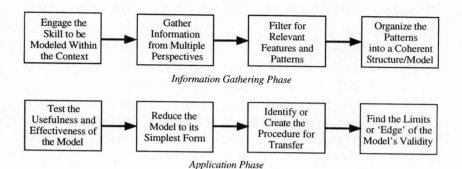

Information Gathering Phase

Application Phase

Flow Chart of the Basic Steps of the Modeling Process

Some Beginning Modeling Drills and Exercises

The purpose of the following exercises is to provide some experience with the basic processes and procedures of modeling. They primarily focus on the information gathering phase of the modeling process, and cover a range of modeling skills, including "implicit" and "explicit" modeling formats, and the use of multiple perceptual positions to gather different types and levels of information about a particular performance.

Mirroring Exercise

Mirroring is a method of building a strong "second position" with someone else. It is a fundamental skill for modeling another person and for developing intuitions about the person's internal experience. To get a sense of the influence and effects of mirroring, try out the following exercise.

1. Choose a partner, or person to converse with. Do not tell the person initially that you will be mirroring him or her during the conversation.
2. Enter into a conversation with the person, asking for his or her opinions about various subjects.
3. As you are conversing, begin to subtly mirror the other person's physiology (including voice tone and tempo). [Hint: This can be most easily done in the context of 'active listening'; that is, reflecting back statements the person has made, by commenting, "So what you are saying is....", and then stating your understanding of the person's opinion.]
4. When you are fully mirroring, you will be sitting in the same posture, using the same types of gestures, speaking at a similar speed and volume, and in a similar voice tone range, as the other person. If you are completely

mirroring the other person, you will even be breathing at the same rate and in the same part of the chest cavity as the other. Notice what it feels like when you have reached this level of rapport.

5. One way to test your degree of rapport is by "second guessing" the other person's opinion on a couple of subjects that you have not yet discussed. Often mirroring will give you access to information that is being unconsciously communicated and received, and you will "pick up" information about the other person without being consciously aware of how you got it. This is why mirroring is such a powerful tool for modeling.

6. To get another sense of the influence of mirroring on your interaction, you can try out what it is like to abruptly mismatch the other person in posture, gestures, voice tone and breathing. Both you and your partner should experience quite a jolt if you do this, and feel as if your quality of rapport has changed dramatically.

7. Before concluding your conversation and letting your partner in on what you were doing, make sure you have reestablished rapport by once again physically mirroring your partner.

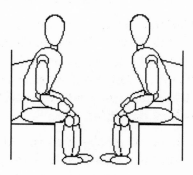

Mirroring Involves Matching the Physical Patterns of Another Person

"Implicit" Modeling from Second Position

This exercise is to be done with four persons: (1) the
Person to be modeled, (2) a Subject to interact with the
individual being modeled, (3) a Modeler, and (4) an Observer

1. The Subject and the Person to be modeled engage in a
   conversation (for approximately 5 minutes) about a
   topic, chosen by the Person being modeled. The Modeler
   "implicitly" models the Person by going to 'second position' with the Person, and focusing on the micro muscle
   movements of the individual.

2. The Modeler then 'stands in' for the Person he or she has
   been modeling – i.e., the Modeler continues the conversation with the Subject "as if" he or she were that Person.

3. The Modeler is to receive explicit feedback and coaching
   by the Person being modeled and the Observer about
   how accurately he or she is acting like the Person being
   modeled. (If the Modeler experiences difficulty, repeat
   steps 1 & 2 another time.)

4. The Modeler is then sent out of the room, and the
   Subject and the Person being modeled converse about a
   different topic (5 min.), chosen by the Subject this time.

5. When the Modeler returns, he or she is to once again
   "stand in" for the Person being modeled, and converse
   with the Subject about the new topic "as if" he or she
   were that Person. (The Subject should try to replicate
   the order of the questions and interaction of the conversation as much as possible.)

6. After about 5 minutes, the Subject, Observer and the
   Person who has been modeled are to give the Modeler
   feedback as to how accurately his or her performance
   matched that of the Person being modeled.

Building Double and Triple Descriptions Through 'Co-Modeling'

The process of Co-Modeling involves the participation of two people in the modeling process to build a "double-description" and "triple-description" of the process to be modeled. Co-Modeling allows for the immediate intertwining of both the explicit and implicit modeling processes. In much the same way that our two eyes see depth by giving us a 'double-description' of the visual world around us, Co-Modeling gives depth to the modeling process by providing multiple simultaneous perspectives of the same subject.

These exercise are to be done in groups of three (**A, B & C**): **A** = Person to be Modeled; **B & C** = Modelers.

Co-Modelers

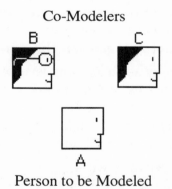

Person to be Modeled

Exercise 1: Building Intuitions Using Second Position

1. Person A demonstrates a simple behavioral skill to be modeled (e.g., a dance step, a culturally related gesture or greeting, entering a particular resource state, etc.).

2. Persons B & C go into a state of "not knowing," and enter into 'second position' with A for a few minutes.

3. B & C then write down explicitly what they think is going on in A based on their implicit experience gained from 'second position'.

4. B & C compare their models, identifying similarities and differences between their two descriptions.

5. A, B & C then work together to create a "triple description" of the key elements of the behavioral skill demonstrated by A.

Exercise 2: "Explicit Modeling" Using Third Position

1. Person A demonstrates a simple behavioral skill to be modeled.

2. Staying in a 'third position', or 'observer' position, persons B & C have 10 minutes to elicit verbal information and behavioral demonstrations from A, in order to get explicit information about the skill being modeled.

   (Note: B & C may ask about any level of information— i.e., physiology, representational systems, language patterns, T.O.T.E., meta programs, beliefs, etc. They can explore any level of information they think will provide the most useful information about the skill being modeled.)

3. B & C then write down explicitly what they think is going on inside A, based on their observations and the information that they have elicited.

4. B & C compare their models, identifying similarities and differences between the two descriptions.

5. Again, persons A, B & C work together to create a third description of the key elements of the behavioral skill demonstrated by A.

Notice the different dynamics and quality of information that comes from the two exercises.

Exercise 3: Modeling States of Excellence Combining Second and Third Position

1. Person A selects and demonstrates an example of a personal resource state, or "state of excellence."

2. Person B models A implicitly, using 2nd position.

3. Person C models A explicitly, from 3rd position. C asks 'why' questions which address beliefs, values, meta programs, meta-outcomes; and 'how' questions which address goals, evidences and operations (the T.O.T.E. distinctions).

4. Person A now chooses an experience which is opposite to the first example (i.e., a "stuck state").

5. B & C repeat steps 2 and 3 above.

6. B & C compare and contrast their own models of A's examples of excellence and its opposite, and explore what is similar and what is different about their descriptions.

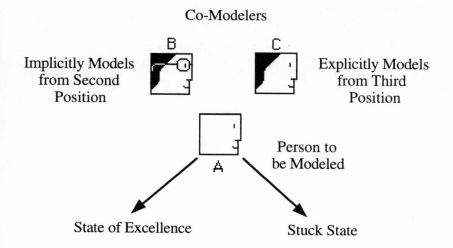

Co-Modelers

B   C

Implicitly Models from Second Position   Explicitly Models from Third Position

A

Person to be Modeled

State of Excellence   Stuck State

Group Modeling

The process of co-modeling can be generalized to an entire group. The following is an exercise that allows a whole group to get involved in the modeling process, and form a "triple description."

1. The group selects a skill from a trainer, or from another person (from outside group), that the group is interested in learning or knowing more about.

2. The group divides into two teams A & B. Team A uses 2nd position, and team B uses 3rd position, to develop descriptions of the skill to be modeled.

3. The person to be modeled demonstrates several examples of the skill, and each team generates a description, using the position they have been assigned. Members of the 3rd position team (B) may choose to focus on different levels of distinctions (physiology, language patterns, cognitive strategies, beliefs, etc.) in order to form their descriptions.

4. Team delegates then summarize the findings and descriptions of their teams to the rest of the group, and the whole group synthesizes the descriptions into a common model.

Finding Relevant Patterns

To go into more depth in the application phase of the modeling process – in which you design, test, and refine your explicit model, and then make it transferrable to others – it is helpful to have some additional distinctions. A particular capability, regardless of its level of sophistication or complexity, is made up of several dimensions relating to the functions defined by the T.O.T.E. A successful performance of any type, for instance, requires the capacities to conceptualize, analyze, observe, follow procedures, interact with others, and manage relationships, to some degree.

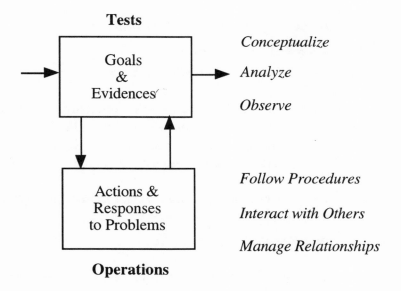

There are Various Dimensions of any Capability Relating to the Functions of the T.O.T.E.

Conceptualization, analysis and observation, are necessary to make effective "Tests." They relate to establishing goals and determining evidences for success. Following procedures, interacting with others and managing relationships, are aspects of the "Operations" necessary to effectively reach the goals and satisfy the evidences that make up the "Test" phase of a particular T.O.T.E. To have a 'complete' model of a particular capability would involve defining each of these various dimensions of the skill to be studied:

a. **Conceptualization** – the ability to conceptualize the whole and relate or fit something into that larger framework. Modeling the *conceptual* dimension of a particular skill or capability relates to answering the questions:

> *What is the purpose of the skill or ability?*
>
> *When would you use it? In which circumstances?*
>
> *How does it fit with other competencies?*

b. **Analysis** – the ability to break something into its component pieces; to categorize its elements. Modeling the *analytical* dimension of a particular skill or capability relates to answering the questions:

> *What distinctions are the most relevant to successfully perform this skill?*
>
> *What do those distinctions indicate?*

c. **Observation** – the ability to gather relevant information in "real time" (often in the form of non-verbal signs). Modeling the *observational* dimension of a particular skill or capability relates to answering the questions:

> *What is most relevant to observe for in order to successfully perform this skill?*

What, specifically, do you need to be able to observe? What cues (or patterns of cues) are most important?

When is it most important to observe for those patterns of cues?

d. **Following Procedures** – the ability to recall and enact a sequential set of steps that lead to an objective. Modeling the *procedural* dimension of a particular skill or capability relates to answering the questions:

What are the key sequences of actions necessary in order to successfully perform this skill? At what level or 'chunk size' are they? i.e., If you were to chunk the ability into a sequence of steps, what would they be?

When and where is it important to follow the sequence precisely? When and where is it important to be flexible?

To what degree do particular steps rely on specific observation?

e. **Interacting with Others** – the ability to systematically elicit and react to the ongoing behavioral responses in others. Modeling the *interactive* dimension of a particular skill or capability relates to answering the questions:

Which possible reactions (on your own part) go with which actions initiated by others? What is the intended result of those reactions?

What particular actions (on your own part) are intended to elicit particular reactions from others? What is the desired result of those reactions?

What cues let you know when it is time to act, react or change actions?

f. **Managing Relationships** – the ability to recognize and select appropriate behavior in relation to role, norms, context, etc. Modeling the *relational* dimension of a particular skill or capability relates to answering the questions:

Under which conditions (contextual, cultural, relational, personal, etc.) is it important to vary the pattern of interaction?

How does the internal state, of either yourself or the others, influence or alter what you do or how you do it?
What desired state(s), within both yourself and others, is the intended result of the procedure or interaction?

Types of Skills	Skill Dimensions					
	Conceptual *When, where and why do you use it?*	**Analytical** *What distinctions are important?*	**Observational** *What cues are necessary to attend to?*	**Procedural** *What sequence of steps must be followed?*	**Interactive** *What actions, reactions and results are most important?*	**Relational** *In what circumstances and situations should you vary your actions?*
Simple Behavioral						
Simple Cognitive						
Simple Linguistic						
Complex Behavioral						
Complex Cognitive						
Complex Linguistic						

A 'complete' model of a particular capability would involve defining all of these various dimensions needed to successfully perform the skill.

Getting the answers to these questions also helps you to determine what will need to be taught or provided in order to transfer the capability to others, and what will be the evidence that the capability has been successfully transferred.

It is not always possible to obtain the answers to these questions, of course, by simply asking the person being modeled and waiting for his or her conscious response. Usually, the best answers are obtained by using the steps of the modeling methodology described earlier (or through the various Modeling Strategies described in the next chapter). One of the greatest challenges in this process, however, occurs at the phase in which you are trying to make an explicit description of the patterns you have discovered. Finding relevant patterns involves two key processes: (a) feature detection and (b) pattern recognition.

A. Feature Detection

Features are the specific qualities or characteristics that we decide to filter for as we are modeling. In NLP, this would include characteristics such as the sensory representational systems someone uses (vision, hearing, feeling, etc.), subtle physical reactions such as eye movements or other accessing cues, linguistic patterns (sensory predicates, Meta Model patterns, etc.), and so on.

The features we choose to look for, of course, determine the kind of patterns we will find. Thus, they will determine to a large degree what we will discover, and how effective our finished model will be. In exploring different types of capabilities we can consider features and characteristics that occur on many different levels.

To effectively model complex human patterns we must keep in mind that not only are there important characteristics in someone's environment and physical behavior, but also in the mental maps that one makes to guide his or her behavior in that environment. These mental maps form the basis for the cognitive strategies by which we select particular behaviors to engage in. At another level, our beliefs and values reinforce and select particular mental capabilities. At a higher level still our identities consolidate our beliefs into a belief system. We will rule out certain beliefs and priorities, for example, because of our cultural or personal identity.

The most common 'features' or distinctions attended to in the NLP modeling process include:

1. **Physiology** – *Observing for physical build, postural patterns, gestures, symmetry and quality of movement, eye movements and other accessing cues, including non-verbal patterns such as voice tone and tempo. (The B.A.G.E.L. Model)*

2. **Cognitive Strategies** – *Observing for any emphasis on particular sensory representational systems, submodality patterns, and habitual cognitive sequences. (The R.O.L.E. Model)*

3. **Meta-Program Patterns** – *Observing for general organizational patterns such as time perception and management, relationships to significant others, orientations towards goals, etc.*

4. **Belief and Value Systems** – *Observing for any stated values, rules, attitudes or presuppositions about the behavior or skill to be modeled.*

5. **Meta-Patterns** – *Observing the interaction between the individual being modeled and the other people that individual is involved with in the situation you are modeling. Note any patterns in the way the individual being modeled communicates or relates to the others involved in the situation.*

Of course, some of these distinctions will be more relevant to modeling certain types of capabilities than others. Simple behavioral modeling, for instance, will most likely involve an emphasis on specific patterns of physiology. Modeling simple cognitive capabilities, on the other hand, generally involves an emphasis on representational systems and submodalities. The modeling of a complex behavioral capability would require more emphasis on interactive 'meta patterns', and so on. The following is a list of the types of NLP distinctions most commonly related to the level of capability that is the focus of a particular modeling project:

a) Simple Behavioral – *Specific physical cues and actions (the B.A.G.E.L. Model)*

b) Simple Cognitive – *Representational Systems and Submodalities (the R.O.L.E. Model)*

c) Simple Linguistic – *Meta Model Patterns and Predicates*

d) Complex Behavioral – *S.C.O.R.E. Model Distinctions and Perceptual Positions*

e) Complex Cognitive – *SOAR Model Distinctions, Meta Program Patterns and Logical Levels*

f) Complex Linguistic – *Communication Matrix Distinctions and Sleight of Mouth Patterns*

B. Pattern Recognition

In modeling, *pattern recognition* refers to the processes or procedures used to identify the particular features or distinctions that are the most important for achieving a particular goal or result. The most fundamental way to accomplish this is to find a group of individuals who are already able to demonstrate the desired capability, or achieve the desired result, and find the similarities and differences between them with respect to the features or characteristics you have chosen to explore. The goal of modeling is not to find the 'average' behavior of these models, but rather to determine what specific features are common to the processes used by all of the individuals being modeled.

Finding patterns is different than simply identifying features. The fact that a person is able to see and categorize eye movements, for example, is not the same as determining which of those eye movements (if any) are essential for a certain skill or capability. Pattern recognition involves identifying consistent or repetitive features in some performance that are key elements in enacting the particular capability or achieving a particular result. According to Merriam-Webster's Dictionary, a *pattern* is "a reliable sample of traits, acts, tendencies, or other observable characteristics of a person, group, or institution," or "a frequent or widespread incidence."

Mill's Methods

John Stuart Mill, one of the most influential British social and political thinkers of the mid-Victorian period, left a permanent imprint on philosophy through his restatements of the principles underlying philosophical empiricism and utilitarianism. A child prodigy, Mill had mastered Greek by the age of 7 and studied economics at the age of 13. As a defender of individual liberty against state interference, and as an early advocate of women's equality, Mill's ideas continue to be of major significance. Mill's earliest important philosophical work, the *System of Logic* (1843), contains a valuable discussion of the epistemological principles underlying empiricism. In it, Mill defines the five primary strategies or methods in which scientists identify patterns through 'inductive' reasoning. These processes are known as "Mill's Methods" in his honor.

Mill's method of *Agreement* involves observing a series of examples in which a particular result has been achieved, and sorting for which factors or features are the same across all of the instances. Noticing that a group of positive memories all share the quality of having bright and colorful internal images would be an example of "agreement."

In the method of *Difference* one would seek a particular element or feature that has not normally been a part of a situation or phenomenon but is suddenly present in an instance in which a particular result has been achieved. Noticing that, in a series of examples of memories of creative performances, the one that stands out as being "most creative" is different from the others in that the internal image associated with it has the most movement, would be an example of "difference."

The *Joint Method of Agreement and Difference* (known in NLP as "contrastive analysis") involves observing for which features are always present when a particular result is achieved and is always absent when the result is not achieved.

For instance, a person may notice that when he or she is able to successfully achieve a creative state, it is always accompanied by constructed visual images and positive internal dialog. When he or she is unable to reach the state, there are no such images and there is the presence of a critical internal voice.

Mill's fourth method is that of *Concomitant Variation*. This involves noticing features which vary in direct (or inverse) relationship with the <u>degree</u> of success with which the desired result has been achieved. As an example, recognizing that if one increases the vividness of color of one's internal images one feels more creative, but feels less creative if the colors become dull, is applying the method of concomitant variation.

The final Mill's method is that of *Residues* (otherwise known as "the process of elimination"). If a particular feature of a complex phenomenon is observed in association with a particular part of the desired result, then we can assume that the remaining parts of the result will be associated with the remaining features of the phenomenon. Thus, if a person finds a colorful, bright image both creative and motivating, and the "vividness of the colors" is found to be connected to the degree to which the image is experienced as "creative," it is probable that the remaining feature (the "brightness" of the image) will be associated with the feeling of motivation.

Finding counter examples is a common means of applying the method of 'residues'.

Summary of "Mill's Methods"

1. **AGREEMENT** – Observe which feature(s) is present in a series of examples in which the desired result has been achieved (e.g., the "▲" below).

e.g.

FEATURES				*DESIRED RESULT*
❁	❑	▲	⟶	**present**
▲	✖	➔	⟶	**present**
❁	▲	✖	⟶	**present**
❑	▲	✖	⟶	**present**

2. **DIFFERENCE** – Observe a particular feature(s) that has not normally been there but is suddenly present in an instance in which the desired result has been achieved (e.g., the "✔" below).

e.g.

FEATURES				*DESIRED RESULT*
❁	❑	➔	⟶	*absent*
✖	➔	✳	⟶	*absent*
❁	❑	▲	⟶	*absent*
➔	✳	✔	⟶	**present**

3. **JOINT METHOD OF AGREEMENT AND DIFFER-ENCE (CONTRAST)** – Observe which features are always present when the desired result is achieved and always absent when the result is not achieved (e.g., the "❑" in the following example).

e.g.

FEATURES				*DESIRED RESULT*
✿	❑	▲	⟶	**present**
❑	✖	→	⟶	**present**
✿	→	▲	⟶	*absent*
✖	✿	❑	⟶	**present**
▲	✖	→	⟶	*absent*
✖	✿	▲	⟶	*absent*

4. **CONCOMITANT VARIATION** – Observe features which vary in direct (or inverse) relationship with the <u>degree</u> of success which the desired result has been achieved.

e.g.

FEATURES		*DESIRED RESULT*
f —> **F**	⟶	r —> **R**
F —> f	⟶	**R** —> r

5. **RESIDUES (PROCESS OF ELIMINATION)** – If a particular feature of a complex phenomenon is observed in association with a particular part of the desired result, then we can assume that the remaining parts of the result will be associated with the remaining features of the phenomenon.

e.g.

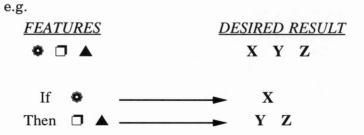

FEATURES		*DESIRED RESULT*
✿ ❑ ▲		X Y Z
If ✿	⟶	X
Then ❑ ▲	⟶	Y Z

Modeling with Mill's Methods

Mill's Methods constitute the basic pattern finding processes in NLP modeling procedures, and is the conceptual framework behind NLP strategies and techniques such as Submodality Utilization, Mapping Across, and State Management. To get a sense for how Mill's Methods are applied to modeling, try out the following simple examples of pattern finding using the various Mill's Methods. (Some possible answers are provided at the end of the exercise.)

1. **Agreement:** A person is asked to make a decision regarding four different financial investments. The drawings below show the posture taken by the individual as he or she makes each decision. What is the *same* about each posture?

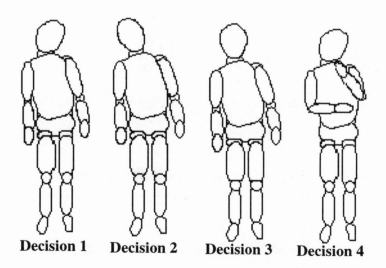

Decision 1   **Decision 2**   **Decision 3**   **Decision 4**

Mill's Method of Agreement Involves Identifying What is Similar About a Number of Examples

2. **Difference:** A person is asked to recall a particular detail from a complicated visual pattern. The person tries several times to remember, but struggles and is unsuccessful. Finally, on the fourth attempt, the person is able to successfully recall the detail. The following drawings depict the posture of the person during each attempt. What is *different* about the posture during the fourth attempt?

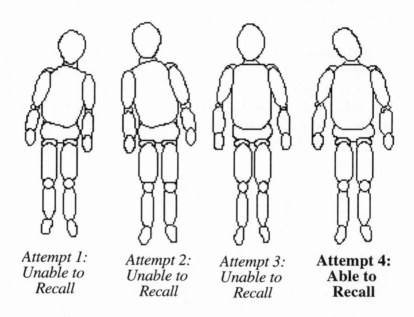

Attempt 1:   Attempt 2:   Attempt 3:   **Attempt 4:**
Unable to   *Unable to*   *Unable to*   **Able to**
Recall   *Recall*   *Recall*   **Recall**

Mill's Method of Difference Involves Identifying What is Different About a Successful Example

3. **Joint Method of Agreement and Difference:** A person is asked to recall and reexperience various instances in which the person was either "stuck" or "creative." The following drawings illustrate the posture of the person as he or she was reexperiencing each

instance. What is the *same* about the creative states? How is the physiology associated with the stuck state *different* from the creative state?

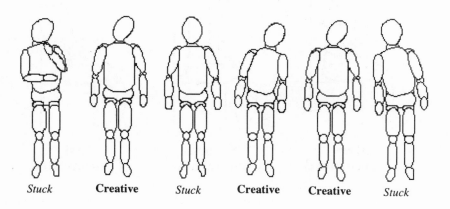

Stuck   **Creative**   *Stuck*   **Creative**   **Creative**   *Stuck*

Mill's Joint Method of Agreement and Difference Involves Identifying What is the Same and Different About Examples Associated with Different Results

4. **Concomitant Variation:** A person is asked to concentrate on a verbal recall task. The person is given various groups of words to remember, which the person must then repeat. Some sets are made up of easy words that rhyme with one another; other sets have more complicated words; and some sets are made up of words from a language that the person is unfamiliar with. The person reports that it requires more concentration to recall and repeat the words from the unfamiliar language, and less concentration to remember the simple word sets. It is observed that the person's posture shifts slightly as he or she is listening to the various word sets, as shown in the following drawings. What feature of the person's posture *varies* with his or her degree of concentration?

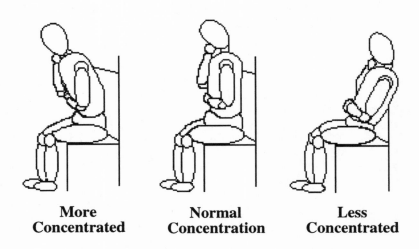

| More
Concentrated | Normal
Concentration | Less
Concentrated |

**Mill's Method of Concomitant Variation Involves
Identifying What Features Change as the Result
Varies**

5. **Residues:** A person enters a "Dreamer" state, and
displays the physical position shown in the drawing
below. The person describes the state as being relaxed,
balanced and involving visual imagination." Through
questioning and observation it is determined that the
person's head and eye position (looking up) are associated with his or her visualizing ability. What other
aspects of the state might be associated with the *remaining* physical features; such as, the person's body
posture (leaning back), and the position of the person's
arms and legs (symmetrical)?

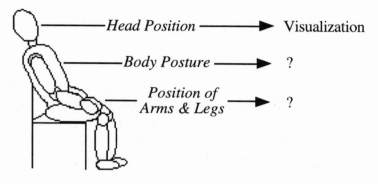

"Dreamer" State:
Relaxed, Balanced, Use of Visualization

According to Mill's Method of Residues, Different Aspects of a Complex Result Come From Different Patterns in the System that Produced the Result

Some possible answers to the exercise questions are:

1. Agreement: The position of the person's legs and pelvis are the same in each example (i.e., symmetrical and stable); and the upper part of the person's body (the torso) is tilted to the person's right.

2. Difference: The person's head is tilted up and to his or her left; and the posture appears to be slightly more erect.

3. Joint Method of Agreement and Difference: In all of the "creative" states, the person's head is tilted up and to his or her right; and the person's weight appears to be placed slightly more on the left leg. The physiology of the "stuck" states differ from the "creative" state physiology in that the head is always in a different position; and the weight of the body appears to be shifted onto the right leg.

4. Concomitant Variation: The position of the person's upper body (torso) varies with the degree of concentration; i.e., the person leans more forward when concentrating more intently, and leans backward when requiring less concentration.

5. Residues: The person's body posture (leaning back) is possibly related to the feeling of "being relaxed;" and the symmetry of the person's arms and legs may be associated with the sense of "balance." To test this hypothesis, the person could be asked to cross one of his or her legs or arms over the other (producing a physical asymmetry) while maintaining an elevated head position and continuing to lean back (as in the following drawing). The person could then be asked what has shifted with respect to the state. If the person reports feeling less "balanced," with one arm crossed over the other, for instance, then it can be assumed that there is a relation between the symmetry of the person's arm position and the person's sense of "balance."

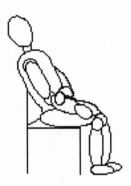

Shifting One Feature, While Holding the Others Constant, Helps to Determine What Impact That Feature Has On the Results

Possible Fallacies in the Mill's Methods

When modeling, it is important to always keep in mind that no single pattern finding method is foolproof. Mill's methods are ways to identify potential patterns. Each method is subject to "fallacies" if taken as a "proof" on its own. Mill's method of Agreement, for instance, can produce the type of errors exemplified by the "logical drinker." The logical drinker claims, "I had five whiskey and sodas on Monday and woke up with a terrible hangover. So the next night I switched and had five Scotch and sodas, but I still woke up the next morning with a terrible hangover. So I switched again the next night and had five bourbon and sodas, but I was just as sick the next morning. Tonight I'm going to just take my whiskey straight. That darn soda is causing me too many hangovers."

The Mill's method of Difference, if applied exclusively, can produce the type of thinking that creates superstitions. For instance, let's say a person has purchased many lottery tickets without winning. Then, one day the person gets the lucky numbers. The person notes that, on that day, he or she happened to be wearing a new pair of green socks, and thinks, "Wow, I'm going to put on these socks and go to Las Vegas to go gambling. They will help me to win a pile of money." While the green socks may have been a definite difference that accompanied the result of winning the lottery, wearing them is not necessarily causally related. The fear of bad luck resulting from breaking a mirror, a black cat crossing one's path, walking under a ladder, or Friday the 13th, etc., are other examples of superstitions that can get started as a result of using Mill's Method of Difference without any other form of testing or verification.

Similarly, the fact that a Contrastive Analysis (the Joint Method of Agreement and Difference) can demonstrate that the main works of genius in the past several centuries can be definitely associated with Caucasian males of European descent does not mean that women or non-Europeans are incapable of genius. Other factors such as cultural support, gender roles, and even definitions of "genius" (what Aristotle would call "formal causes"), may create biases and filters that influence who is recognized as a genius, and who is given the necessary opportunities and encouragement.

Other fallacies can occur in relation to Concomitant Variation. Statisticians, for example, report a correlation between the amount of ice cream people eat and the incidence of drowning. To assume a causal relationship between the two, however, may be jumping to conclusions. Both the amount of ice cream that is eaten and the number of people that go swimming increase during the Summer because the weather is warmer, not necessarily because there is any direct connection between eating ice cream and drowning per se.

The method of Residues (Process of Elimination) is also subject to fallacies. Consider the doctor who says to his or her patient, "Well, there is good news and bad news. The bad news is, nine out of ten patients die from the treatment I am going to recommend. The good news is, my last nine patients died from my treatment, so you must be the lucky tenth person who will survive."

Pattern verification procedures, such as seeking counter examples, and perceiving causal relationships from a more systemic perspective, are necessary to prevent the types of fallacies described above.

Mill's Methods all presuppose the observation of several examples or instances of the phenomenon or performance being examined. In fact, a minimum number of examples is important in order to be able to definitely identify a pattern. From an NLP perspective, that minimum number is three. A feature that appears in one example of a successful performance forms the basis, along with many other possibilities, of a potential pattern. A feature that reoccurs in two examples of successful performances suggests that a particular pattern may, in fact, be present. A feature that is present in three examples begins to become convincing evidence that a pattern does indeed exist.

The ultimate criterion for identifying patterns in modeling, however, is that, when you apply the feature, you are able to achieve the result. A "pattern" cannot truly be tested or evaluated until it is put to use.

Defining a Modeling Project

To summarize, the effective modeling of a particular capability, and the subsequent organization of the results into engineered training programs, techniques and tools, is dependent on the 'features' or distinctions one sorts and filters for, and on the ability to find relevant patterns with respect to those features. The basic sequence of events involved in a modeling project needs to insure that the relevant features and patterns will be found. A typical sequence of steps is:

1. Conducting a needs analysis to determine the specific issues, contexts and skills to be addressed.
2. Selecting the individuals to be modeled.
3. Setting up and carrying out modeling scenarios and procedures in order to engage the capabilities or performance to be examined and gather the necessary information.
4. Identifying relevant patterns in the behavior, strategies and beliefs, etc., of the individuals who have been modeled.
5. Organizing the patterns that have been discovered into a descriptive and prescriptive structure; i.e., a "model."
6. Experimentally testing and refining the model by trying it out in the relevant context(s) to see if it achieves the desired results.
7. Designing effective installation/intervention procedures and tools in order to transfer or apply the key elements of the model to others.
8. Measuring the results obtained by applying the model.

Defining a modeling project involves specifying the basic framework within which the modeling project will take place. The following worksheet can be used to help form an outline of the key dimensions which will shape and guide your modeling project.

Modeling Project Worksheet

1. Write a title or a phrase that defines the essence of your modeling project.

2. What is the capability or result upon which your modeling project is focused? (e.g., leadership, making an effective presentation, spelling, coping with stress, etc.) If there are several related capabilities, or sub-capabilities or results, list all of them. Identify the level of complexity of each skill (i.e, simple behavioral, simple cognitive, simple linguistic, complex behavioral, complex cognitive, or complex linguistic).

3. Who will you be modeling? (You can either list the names of specific people, or define the characteristics of the people that you will need to model.)

4. Are there specific contexts of situations in which you will need to engage and observe the individuals you are modeling? If so, which ones?

5. What are your desired outcomes (goals and objectives) for the modeling project?

6. What are the desired effects of your modeling project? Who will benefit, and in what way? How will it contribute to a larger system or community?

7. What criteria will guide your modeling project and, in particular, the way you intend to apply what you have modeled? (e.g., accepted by a certain profession, profitable, community oriented, fun, etc.)

8. What will be the specific output(s) of your modeling project? (i.e., article, video, book, seminar, etc.)

9. What is your general time frame for completing your modeling project?

Defining Evidence and Evidence Procedures for Project Goals and Outcomes

Defining a modeling project also involves considering certain "epistemological questions" about the criteria and evidence procedures you will be using to test and evaluate the results of the information you will be gathering. *Epistemological questions* are questions relating to "how you know" something. Some of the questions most relevant for modeling include:

Preparation: What criteria will you use (have you used) to identify the individual(s) you will be modeling?

• How do (will) *you* know that the person(s) to be modeled has (have) the desired skill?

• How do (will) *others* know that the person(s) to be modeled has (have) the desired skill?

Phases 1 and 2 (Information Gathering through Implicit and Explicit Modeling): What criteria will you use to know that you have effectively modeled the capability?

• How does the person being modeled know that *he or she* has the desired skill or has achieved the desired result?

• How do (will) *you* know that *you* have learned the skill possessed by the model(s)?

• How will *others* know that *you* have learned the skill possessed by the model(s)?

Phase 3 (Design): What criteria will you use to know you have effectively transferred the capability?

• How will *you* know that *others* have learned the skill possessed by the model(s)?

• How will *others* know that *they* have learned the skill possessed by the model(s)?

Answering these questions will help you to determine and design the most effective modeling procedures.

Goals for the Modeling Process

In conclusion, the overall goal of modeling is to create a practical map of a particular capability or skill by breaking it into "chunks" and identifying the relevant features and steps that are necessary in order to apply that capability in some way. The purpose of applying a particular model, or doing a particular modeling activity, may be to either:

a) Learn about differences

b) Do something differently

c) Do something better

d) Do something new

e) Have more choices

f) Transform perceptions

As NLP co-founder Richard Bandler pointed out, the process of modeling is the true essence of NLP, not the trail of techniques that has been left in its wake.

Modeling is a classic example of "double loop learning." There is an old adage which states that "if you give a person a fish, you have fed him for a day; but if you teach a person how to fish, you have fed him for the rest of his life." "Double loop learning" would involve helping a person to catch a fish, and in doing so, teaching the person how to fish at the same time. It involves achieving two simultaneous outcomes – learning *what* to do and, at the same time, *how* to do it.

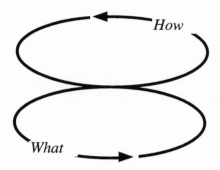

Double Loop Learning Involves Two Simultaneous Levels of Learning

In a company or organization, for instance, the process of an individual or group that does something effectively can be modeled, so that the structure of their process can be made explicit and taught to other individuals and groups. At the same time, that group can learn the process of *how to model*. So, not only do they receive the benefit of the results of the modeling project, they learn how to model on their own at the same time. Thus, people are able to develop the skills of modeling by applying them to concrete experiences.

This type of "double loop" process serves multiple purposes in that it:

- is more cost effective
- brings the resources internal to the company or organization
- guarantees long term systemic change

Because it provides more value and saves time, more and more learning processes in the future will have this "double loop" characteristic provided by the process of modeling.

Chapter 4

Modeling
Strategies

Overview of Chapter 4

- **Modeling Strategies**
- **Micro Modeling Strategies**
  - **T.O.T.E. Questionnaire**
- **Macro Modeling Strategies**
  - **Multi-Level Modeling Questions**
- **Applied Modeling Strategies**
  - **Applied Modeling Questions**
- **Advanced Modeling Strategy**
- **Applied Modeling and the "Back-Propagation" Process**
- **Code Congruence**

Modeling Strategies

Modeling involves creating a description of a phenomenon or process, that accounts for its "known or inferred properties," and can be used and refined in order to create a final product or service based on that description. The NLP modeling process consists of applying various strategies for examining the mental and physical processes which underlie a particular performance or the achievement of a particular result, and then creating some type of explicit map or description of those processes which can be applied for some practical purpose. Various modeling strategies delineate different sequences of steps and types of distinctions through which relevant patterns may discovered and formed into descriptions.

It should be pointed out that modeling strategies are sub-processes within the overall NLP modeling methodology. The general modeling methodology of NLP involves first developing an intuition base about a particular behavior or capability by "implicitly" modeling (primarily through "second position") the persons who possess the necessary skills, until one can achieve the desired results. The second phase involves "explicitly" identifying and defining which characteristics and patterns are most relevant for achieving those desired results. The final phase of modeling involves designing the procedures and tools through which those patterns and characteristics can best be transferred to others. Modeling strategies are primarily applied during the "explicit" modeling phase and to facilitate the design of transfer procedures.

Modeling strategies involve both inductive and deductive processes. *Inductive* processes are those through which we perceive patterns in the world around us. *Deductive* processes are those through which we describe and act on our perceptions. It is a different process, for example, to be able to understand a language than to speak it. In modeling, the distinction between inductive and deductive strategies relates to the distinction between the "uptake" or information gathering phase and the application phase of the overall modeling process.

While all NLP modeling processes share common features, certain modeling strategies can be more efficient or useful than others, depending on the type of capability or performance to be modeled, the level of complexity involved in that capability or performance, and the stage one is at in the modeling process. The following is a summary of some of the basic modeling strategies used to elicit, organize and apply relevant patterns from an individual or group of individuals who are able to demonstrate some capability or perform effectively.

Micro Modeling Strategies

Micro Modeling Strategies involve modeling the pieces of a specific skill (i.e., a simple behavioral, simple cognitive or simple linguistic ability; such as a particular presentation skill).

1. Identify the skill you want to find out about.

2. Have the person to be modeled demonstrate an example of that skill in a specific context.

3. Elicit the person's T.O.T.E. for applying the skill in that context.

**'Micro Modeling' Involves Eliciting the T.O.T.E.
Structure of a Particular Performance**

T.O.T.E. Modeling Questions

1. What is a context in which you commonly use the skill to be modeled?

2. What are the goals or objectives that guide your actions as you apply the skill in this context? (List them in short sentences or key words.)

3. What do you use as evidence to know that you are accomplishing those goals?

4. What do you do to get to the goals – what are some specific steps and activities that you use to achieve your goals in this context?

5. When you experience unexpected problems or difficulties in achieving your goals in this context, what specific activities or steps do you take to correct them?

Example: Modeling Presentation Skills·

1. A Presenter (the person to be modeled) makes a short presentation (3-5 minutes) to a group of three, on a topic of his or her choice.

2. Each group member identifies and states a specific, simple behavioral pattern they would like to model with respect to the Presenter's performance.

3. The group elicit's the Presenter's T.O.T.E. for the presentation (i.e., his or her goals, evidence and operations) to give a context to the behavior pattern.

4. Each group member has 20 minutes to model the desired behavior pattern, using a modeling procedure of his or her choice.

5. After the behavior has been successfully modeled and demonstrated by a particular group member, the group member is to explore the questions: "How does this pattern affect me on other levels beyond the specific behavior?" "What seem to be the assumptions and presuppositions behind this behavior?"

Macro Modeling Strategies

Macro Modeling Strategies involve identifying the component skills of a more complex or involved ability (i.e., complex behavioral, complex cognitive or complex linguistic), such as "Leadership."

1. Engage the person(s) to be modeled in a context which requires the ability.

2. Identify specific behavioral examples and demonstrations of the ability to be modeled.

3. Starting with the behavior elicit the various levels of processes (how, why and who) that support the behavior.

'Macro Modeling' Involves Chunking a Complex Ability into the Various Levels of Process that are Necessary to Produce It

Multi-Level Modeling Questions

With a partner or group, identify the behavior pattern to be modeled. Starting at the level of behavior, elicit the rest of the supporting logical levels associated with that behavior.

1. "What is the context or *environment* you are exploring?"

   "*When* and *where* does the capability or activity to be modeled occur?"

   The context in which the capability occurs is

   _____

2. "What are the specific *behaviors* associated with the capability that you are exploring? What aspects of the behavior are particularly significant in order to achieve the desired result?

   "*What*, specific behaviors are essential to the process to be modeled?"

   (Create or simulate an example of the context in which the behavior occurs in order to get an ongoing demonstration of the ability to be modeled. This is necessary in order to ground or anchor the following questions in something concrete, and prevent the answers from being simply "theorizing.")

3. "What internal thoughts and *capabilities* are associated with that behavior?"

   "*How* do you think when you are acting in that way? What cognitive processes are behind or presupposed by the behavior you defined and demonstrated during step 2?"

The thoughts and capabilities I associate with the behavior are

_____

4. "What _beliefs_ and _values_ are expressed by or validated by the thoughts and actions you have defined?"

   "What values are expressed by your behavior and capabilities?"

I value

_____

   "_Why_ do those particular thoughts and behaviors express your values? What beliefs provide the motivation for your thoughts and activity?"

I believe

_____

5. "What is your perception of _identity_ or role with respect to your thoughts and actions and the beliefs and values associated with them?" (It is often useful to use a metaphor here as well as a literal description.)

   "_Who_ are you if you engage those particular beliefs, values, capabilities and behaviors?"

I am (or am like)

_____

"What is your mission?" "Who else are you serving with this activity?"

My mission is to

_____

6. "What is your sense of the *larger system* in which you are operating?"

"What is your *vision* of the larger system in which you are pursuing that mission?"

This mission is in the service of the larger vision to

_____

Example 'Macro Modeling' Exercise

1. Locate a space representing the context in which the person to be modeled manifests "X" (i.e., leadership, creativity, learning, etc.). Have the person enter this space and, from 1st position, experience the process of scanning and monitoring an environment in which he or she is able to do "X". Find the beliefs and values which guide the person in this context.

2. Locate another space for a context in which the person is not able to manifest "X". Find the beliefs and values which are different in this context.

3. Have the person return to each of these positions and, from each one, move to action, or see the next steps he or she would take, as well as the longer term consequences related to those actions and steps.

4. Establish a new location for a third position in which the person to be modeled can view both the effective and ineffective contexts. From this perspective, evaluate the similarities and the differences between the first and second contexts with respect to the beliefs, values, and anticipated consequences.

5. Add a fourth position, from which to consider all three of the other perspectives. From here, evaluate the presuppositions operating in the evaluations that were made in the third position space. Are they appropriate? How did you select what constituted a creativity, learning or leadership context? What did you presuppose about the beliefs and values in those contexts? etc.

Applied Modeling Strategies

Applied Modeling Strategies involve (a) identifying the key capabilities possessed by individuals who are able to achieve a particular result or outcome, (b) specifying the particular individuals who may benefit from being able to learn those capabilities and achieve those results, and (c) defining which of those capabilities are most needed by the individuals who require the skill or desire to achieve the results. A common approach to applied modeling is to first identify a need or problem to be addressed, and then to find or select individuals who possess the capabilities or resources necessary to effectively deal with the need or problem. Another approach would first involve identifying the capabilities possessed by individuals who are able to achieve a particular outcome, and then to identify the group of individuals who could most benefit from those capabilities.

Applied modeling also involves putting the identified capabilities into a form such that they can be developed and internalized by the people who need them (such as a Spelling Strategy, an Allergy Technique, Tools for Weight Management, a Leadership Seminar, an Addiction Treatment Plan, etc.).

In many ways, applied modeling involves putting the information gathered from the other modeling strategies into practice. This involves structuring the information gathering process in a "Present State – Desired State" format known as the S.C.O.R.E. Model. The S.C.O.R.E. distinctions define the essential features of a particular "problem space": the *symptoms* associated with the Present (or Problem) State; the *causes* of those symptoms; the desired *outcome* which would replace the symptoms; the longer term *effects* of achieving the outcome; and the *resources* necessary to transform the symptoms and their causes, and to achieve the desired outcome and effects. Typically, with respect to modeling, the symptoms and causes (the Present State) are embodied by the individuals who need or desire the capability to be modeled. The outcome, effects and resources are embodied by the individuals to be modeled. It is possible, however, for all of the aspects of the S.C.O.R.E. to be present in the same individual (as in the case of a person who has had a problem or illness, but has been able to overcome it on his or her own).

A basic applied modeling strategy would involve:

1. Identify the full S.C.O.R.E. defining the problem space to be addressed by the modeling project.

2. Elicit:

   a. A Multi-level description of the problem state of the individual(s) who need the resource being modeled.

   b. A Multi-level description of the capabilities of the individuals who possesses the resources necessary to reach the desired state.

3. Transfer the relevant level(s) of the resource possessed by the successful individuals to the individual(s) needing those abilities. (Depending on the level and type of resource, this may involve anchoring, behavioral practice, rehearsal of a particular cognitive sequence or strategy, a set of steps forming a procedure, etc.)

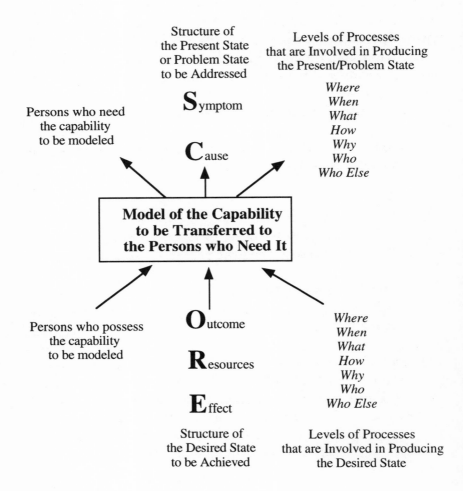

**Applied Modeling Involves Defining the Capabilities
to be Modeled and Transferred to the Individuals Who
Need Them**

Applied Modeling Questions

1. *Symptoms:* What are the specific, observable or measurable symptoms to be addressed by the modeling project?

2. *Causes:* What are the causes of those symptoms?

3. *Outcomes:* What is the outcome or desired state to be reached, that the individual(s) to be modeled is (are) able to demonstrate consistently?

4. *Effects:* What are the longer term positive effects that will be achieved by reaching this outcome?

5. *Resources:* What resources do(es) the person(s) being modeled have that allow him/her/them to: (a) consistently reach the desired outcome, (b) deal effectively with the symptoms, (c) address and transform the causes of the symptom, and (d) move in the direction of the longer term positive effects?

   Identify the resources which are needed by the individuals who are to benefit from the modeling project, and which are possessed by the individual(s) to be modeled, by gathering information at the following levels:

<u>To Be Elicited From the Individuals Who Need the Resource</u>

a. *Environment:* Are there any contextual or environmental constraints with which the individuals who need the capability must contend?

b. *Behavior:* What specific behaviors do the individuals who need the capability currently engage in? i.e., What are the problem behaviors?

b. *Cognitive Capabilities:* What specific capabilities or cognitive strategies do the individuals who need the capability lack, or have that causes them trouble?

d. *Beliefs:* What beliefs do the individuals who need the capability have which either limit or disempower them?

e. *Values:* What values, or hierarchy of values, are the individuals who need the capability operating from?

f. *Sense of Identity:* How do the individuals who need the capability perceive themselves? What is their "self concept?"

g. *Mission and Vision:* Do the individuals who need the capability have any sense of mission or vision with which to organize their activity?

To Be Elicited From the Individuals Who Possess the Resource

a. *Environment:* Are there any contextual or environmental opportunities that the person(s) being modeled has?

b. *Behavior:* What specific observable behaviors are demonstrated by the person(s) being modeled, that are different from that of the individuals who need the capability?

c. *Cognitive Capabilities:* What specific mental capabilities or cognitive strategies are employed by the person(s) being modeled?

d. *Beliefs:* What beliefs do the person(s) being modeled have that allow them to cope more effectively?

e. *Values:* What values, or hierarchy of values, do the person(s) being modeled operate from?

f. *Sense of Identity:* How do the person(s) being modeled perceive themselves?

g. *Mission and Vision:* What type of vision and mission do the person(s) being modeled use to organize their activity?

Advanced Modeling Strategy

Many of the various aspects and phases of the NLP modeling process (including both 'feature detection' and 'pattern recognition', and various elements of the micro, macro and applied modeling strategies) are summarized in the following "Advanced Modeling Strategy," developed by the author.

1. Identify the desired skill or capability to be modeled, and the individual(s) who possess(es) that capability.

2. Set up a situation or context in which you can elicit at least **three** (3) **different specific examples** of the person(s) to be modeled performing the desired skill.

　　a. Elicit the **critical factors** in each of the examples by applying the following perceptual filters:

　　　　1) *Accessing Cues*
　　　　2) *Language Patterns - Meta Model, Predicates, etc.*
　　　　3) *Physiology*
　　　　4) *Representational Systems, Strategies & Submodalities*
　　　　5) *Meta Program Patterns*
　　　　6) *Beliefs and Values*
　　　　7) *Logical Levels*

　　b. Determine which factors are the **same** in all three examples.

3. Find at least one *Counter Example* – *i.e., another person or other persons (including yourself) who is (are) unable to adequately perform the skill,* **or** *situations in which the model was unable to adequately perform the skill.*

Determine the **critical factors of the Counter Example(s)**, applying the same filters used in **Step 2a.**

4. Contrast the critical factors in the 3 successful examples with the critical factors of the Counter-Example(s).

Note the **most significant differences.**

5. *Change* all of the significant critical factors of the Counter-Example(s) to **match** the significant critical factors of the successful examples until you are able to attain the desired behavior or results in the individuals or situations making up the Counter-Example(s).

If changing these factors does not lead to the desired behavior or result, with respect to the individual(s) or situation(s) making up the Counter Example, then *find other more appropriate or powerful examples to model* and continue to repeat the process from **Step 4** until the desired behavior or results are reached.

6. Now begin to vary the critical factors that have contributed to achieving the desired behavior or results, one at a time.

a. Find *"the edge"* by identifying how far you can change the factor before it changes the result.

b. *"Elegance principle"* find the minimum number of factors necessary in order to still achieve the desired behavior or results.

Applied Modeling and the "Back-Propagation" Process

The final stage, the "testing" stage, of both applied modeling and the Advanced Modeling Strategy, is similar to what is known as "back-propagation" in neural network technology. Neural networks are computer structures, based on the way in which the brain functions. They are used to recognize complex patterns. They typically involve a number of interconnected elements that are used to create a type of "model" of some pattern or phenomenon. The model is formed as a function of the "weights," or strengths, of the connections between the elements in the network. This inner "model" determines the output of the network.

The value of neural networks is that they can learn to recognize patterns "heuristically," as a function of repeated experiences. The model (or pattern of "weightings") is adjusted, according to a particular learning rule, each time the network is exposed to a certain input. In this way, the network becomes better and better able to recognize and respond to that particular input; in the same way a child learns to recognize a face or a word. These types of computer networks are commonly used to train audio "voice recognition" systems and optical "character recognition" systems.

A common learning strategy for such networks is "back-propagation." Let's say the computer is being trained to recognize the letters of the alphabet, so that it could read printed documents and translate them into the appropriate computer text characters. To learn to recognize the letter "S," for example, an image of the letter would be input into the network. That image would become coded as a pattern of reactions in the computer network (based on the current "weightings" of its interconnections). As a product of this pattern, the network will output a result – the character "§," for example. The computer's result is compared to the desired result which is expected from the system (i.e., the letter "S"). If there is a discrepancy between the two results —the expected result ("S") and the one produced by the computer ("§")—the weightings between the elements making up the network are adjusted. The image is then input again and the result is tested in the same way. After a number of such cycles, the computer's output begins to more and more match the desired result (that is, the computer outputs the text character "S" when shown the image of the "S"). In other words, the computer has made a useful "model"; it has created a process which achieves the desired result given a particular input.

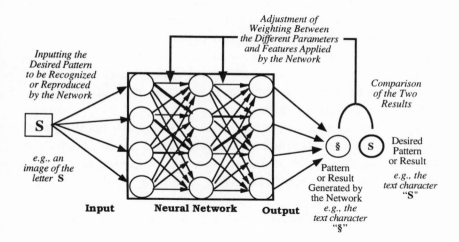

Map of "Back-Propagation" Process in a Neural Network

A similar strategy is used in NLP in order to refine a particular model after it has been established through the various methods and strategies described previously. A human being is a complex "neural network," which can process many different features and distinctions (i.e., Representational Systems, Submodalities, Meta Program Patterns,

Micro Behavioral Cues, language patterns, etc.). Focusing one's "attention" on a particular distinction is like the process of giving "weight" to an element in a computer neural network. For example, telling someone to "put your eyes up and to the left," while that person is attempting to learn to spell a word, would put more "weight" on eye position as a part of effective spelling.

Thus, the steps of a model or procedure direct a person's attention to different aspects and features of his or her experience. This placement of attention creates a type of "attractor" that stimulates "self-organizing" behavior in the person. Noticing the way a tennis ball hits the ground as it is coming toward you, for example, will automatically influence the way you swing your racket in order to return it. Similarly, listening to the changes in a person's tone of voice as opposed to attending to the content of the words a person is using, or, observing a person's facial expressions as opposed to the type of clothes the person is wearing, will alter the way you respond to that person.

The instructions and procedures which make up the principles, steps and strategies of a behavioral model, then, are like the weightings in a neural network. Applying the "back-propagation" approach to behavior modeling would involve:

1. Trying out the steps, strategies and distinctions defined by the model, within the appropriate context.

2. Noticing the results achieved, and comparing them to the desired results.

3. Adjusting the steps and distinctions proposed by the model in order to make a "better approximation."

4. Trying out the new adjustments to the model, and continuing to repeat the process until you (or the people for whom the model is intended) can achieve the required "threshold" level of the desired result.

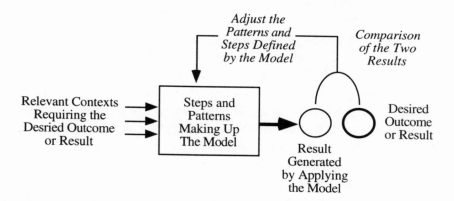

Refining a Technique, Model or Strategy Through the "Back-Propagation" Process

Through this process, the model is refined by applying it experientially. Adjustments are made, as a result of comparing the actual outcome of using the model with the desired outcome, until the most effective and elegant model is produced.

Notice that this approach to evaluating and refining a model is fundamentally different from either simple "feedback" (in which the output of the system is "fed back" as new input), or the attempt to statistically validate a theory by making an analysis of results. "Back-propagation" involves the continual adjustment of the model itself as a function of comparing its output with a desired result.

Code Congruence

According to Gregory Bateson, "If you want to think about something, it is best to think about that thing the same way in which that thing thunk." Bateson's notion of code congruency asserts that the most effective and ecological models are those in which the relationships between the elements within the model match the relationships between the system of elements of the phenomenon which we are modeling.

Bateson points out, for instance, that we can describe a human hand as "five banana shaped objects" or as "four relationships" between adjacent digits. Bateson suggests that one important question is, "Which form of description is more like that used by the DNA and other genetic processes which actually created the hand?" Another question would be, "What difference does it make to think of a hand as four relationships instead of five objects, if we were attempting to make or reproduce one?" Bateson maintains that models which are more "code congruent" are generally more elegant (simpler), useful, and ecological.

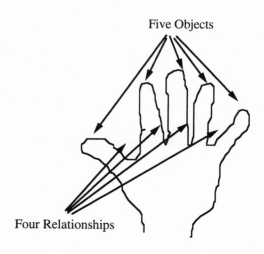

Is a Hand Five Objects Or Four Relationships?

A good example of the value of code congruency in modeling is that of the shift which occurred in the conception framework and mathematics of astronomy in the late Renaissance. Medieval astronomers had assumed that the Earth was the center of the solar system. As a result, they thought that all of the planets revolved around the Earth instead of the sun. In order to describe the orbits of the planets, with the Earth as the center, they had to develop elaborate and complicated mathematical descriptions of the paths traveled by the planets. (When you presuppose that the Earth is the center of the solar system, the planets appear to make strange little sub-loops and 'curly-queues' in their orbits.)

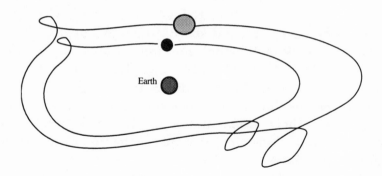

Earth

Paths of the Planets with the Earth Assumed as 'Center' of the Solar System

When the model was finally changed to place the sun at the center of all of their orbits, it became evident that the planets followed relatively simple elliptical paths, and the mathematics required to plot the movement of the planets suddenly became much simpler.

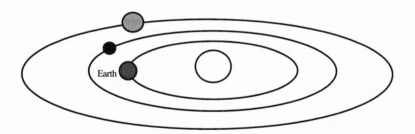

**Paths of the Planets with the Sun Assumed as 'Center'
of the Solar System**

Another example of code congruency from science is the
change that came with Albert Einstein's relativistic approach
to physics. By shifting from the notion of "absolute" time and
space, to relative time and space, Einstein's model was able
to encompass all of Newton's mechanical laws of physics (as
special cases), but was also able to explain and predict more
phenomena; yet require fewer distinctions to do so.

While models that are not code congruent may be useful in
some cases, their scope and longevity is limited. As a
metaphor (and a biological example of the importance of code
congruency), Bateson used to cite the example of an unfertil-
ized frog's egg. An frog's egg is essentially a sphere; and as
such, it is missing quite a bit of the information needed to
become a frog. A sphere has no obvious "front," "back," "left,"
"right," "top, or "bottom." Because the nucleus of the frog's
egg is slightly off center, however, it determines what is to be
the "top" and "bottom" of the frog. In order to begin to turn
into a frog, though, the egg needs information about what is
to be "front," "back," "left" and "right." This information is
usually provided by the entry of the spermatozoan from the
male frog. The place the sperm enters marks the spot that is
to be the front of the frog. If the egg can determine the "top"
and the "front" of the frog, then the "back," "bottom," "left,"
and "right," become obvious.

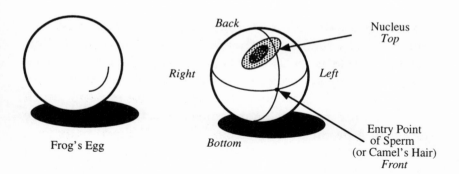

Frog's Egg

Back

Right

Left

Bottom

Nucleus
Top

Entry Point
of Sperm
(or Camel's Hair)
Front

A Camel's Hair is a Type of 'Model' of a Frog's Sperm that is Not Completely 'Code Congruent'

The interesting issue that arises with respect to code congruency comes from the fact that the tip of a camel's hair is about the same size as frog's spermatozoan. If the frog's egg is pricked with the camel's hair, the egg will begin to divide and evolve into a living, breathing, fly catching frog. The camel's hair is a type of "model" of the frog sperm. A frog produced in this manner, however, cannot reproduce, because it is missing the other half of the chromosomes, which would normally be provided by the male's sperm cell (it is what is known as a "haploid"). Thus, the camel's hair is not completely "code congruent" in that it is missing some of the information, or code, necessary to make a fully reproducing frog.

Applying this example as a metaphor for modeling in general, it could be said, in the terms of the NLP Logical Levels model, that camel's hair is able to provide *capability level* information, but does not carry any of the necessary *identity level* information. Thus, one important criterion for "code congruency" in modeling would be to check and include as many different levels of process into a model as possible.

Collateral Energy

Another aspect of code congruency in living systems, emphasized by Bateson, is that of "collateral energy." *Collateral energy* relates to the fact that in many dynamic systems (such as biological and social systems) all of the parts carry their own source of energy. This makes the systems much more complex because energy does not flow through the system in a predictable, mechanical way. Billiard balls on a pool table do not have their own collateral energy, for instance. The energy in such a system is provided by the initial force of the cue stick hitting the cue ball. This energy becomes distributed and dissipated in a predictable manner as each ball hits another.

Gregory Bateson used the analogy of Alice in Wonderland playing a game of croquet using a hedge hog as a ball, and a flamingo as a mallet to express how, when each part of a living system carries its own source of energy, interactions and their results become much more complex and unpredictable. Bateson pointed out that if you kick a ball, you can determine where it will end up with a fair degree of accuracy by calculating the angle of the kick, the amount of force put into the kick, the friction of ground, etc. If you kick a dog, on the other hand, with the same angle, with same force, on the same terrain, etc., it will be much more difficult to predict where it will end up, because the dog has its own "collateral energy."

Newton's laws of physics only partially apply to living systems, whose elements all carry their own collateral energy. Collateral energy is released as a result of difference and information, rather than the initial force put into the system. A very subtle environmental cue can release a great deal of collateral energy. A simple whistle can stimulate a hungry dog to expend a lot of energy to come home for dinner. The wink of an eye from an attractive individual can release quite a bit of energy from an interested suitor. Consider how the abduction of Helen of Troy, lead to many years of war. Similarly, the writings of Karl Marx have stimulated many people to revolution. Beliefs are a good example of how information mobilizes energy.

Many natural scientists still make the error of thinking of living systems as functioning mechanically, rather than as a result of collateral energy. Traditional Western medicine, for example, tends to focus on the mechanical aspects of healing. The Pavlovian notion of the "reflex arc" is an example of applying mechanical thinking to living systems.

Many of the social, political and psychological problems that plague us today are a result of applying mechanical thinking to living systems. The use of force, coercion and manipulation to create social change are examples of ignorance of collateral energy.

Some people even approach NLP methods with a mechanistic perspective. The process of anchoring could be viewed either in terms of mechanical cause-and-effect or as the utilization of collateral energy. The steps of an NLP technique are not like hitting billiard balls on a pool table. Working with people is more like Alice in Wonderland's game of croquet.

Code Congruency in Behavioral Modeling

The importance of applying the principle of code congruency in behavioral modeling can be illustrated in a story coming from the early days of NLP. Bandler and Grinder had decided to conduct a "Modeling Seminar" in which they were to model the work of Virginia Satir. The two-day seminar was structured such that Virginia would work with a family on the first morning, demonstrating her approach to family therapy. In the afternoon, Bandler and Grinder would reflect on her work and describe some of the key linguistic and behavioral patterns that she had applied during the therapy session. Then, the next morning, Virginia would work with another family, leaving the last afternoon for a final reflection and closing remarks.

As the story goes, Virginia did her usual superb job with the family she worked with on the first morning. In the afternoon, Bandler and Grinder proceeded to explain how Virginia had "anchored" various family members using non-verbal cues, how she had led various individuals into certain states, and how she had created and triggered various responses in the family members.

The following morning, when Virginia worked with the next family, it was a disaster. Virginia was unhappy with her work, the family was dissatisfied and the audience was frustrated and confused.

The typical conclusion people draw from this experience is that it can be dangerous to "know what you are doing," because your conscious mind will interfere. Bateson's notion of 'code congruence', however, offers a different explanation. Bandler and Grinder had described Virginia's action in mechanical, cause and effect terms, placing Virginia as the controller of the interaction. Most probably, this was not the way that Virginia herself thought about it, either consciously or unconsciously. From this perspective, her poor performance on the second morning was brought about not merely by the fact that she was conscious of her process, but rather because the code used to model her process was not congruent with the structure of her actual process. [John Grinder relates the story of how, when Bateson first read Bandler and Grinder's work on the *Hypnotic Techniques of Milton Erickson*, Bateson dismissed it with the comment, "Shoddy epistemology," because it had described Erickson's use of language in too mechanical of a manner.]

We have probably all had experiences in which having a way to understand and talk about something we were doing unconsciously and intuitively greatly empowered us and increased our appreciation for and mastery with what we were doing. We have probably also had the experience that knowledge about what we were doing unconsciously brought about a type of self-consciousness which interfered with our ability to perform. Bateson would say that the difference has to do with the congruency of the code being used to the process we are enacting.

When a model is not code congruent, it is like trying to "stick a square peg into a round hole."

Notice that code congruency does not have to do with the "accuracy" of the content of the code or model. A code could be completely metaphorical and still be "congruent" with the process it is representing. The significant aspect of code congruency is that the *relationships* between the elements and events in the model be congruent with the *relationships* between the elements and events making up the system we are modeling.

Chapter 5

Modeling
Leadership Skills

Overview of Chapter 5

- Modeling Leadership Skills at Fiat
- Definition of the Project
- Basic Research Phase
- Applied Research Phase
- General Sequence of Modeling/Installation Activities

Modeling Leadership Skills
At Fiat

In attempting to identify characteristics of effective leaders and leadership, people have examined everything from body language to clothing preferences, to eating habits, to musical taste, and so on. The key to any effective model of behavior, however, is to find those distinctions which are the most fundamental, simple and impactful for producing practical results in the context in which one is operating.

The following account is a summary of a modeling project on effective leadership skills, conducted at Fiat between 1989 and 1993, that illustrates some of the key aspects of the NLP modeling process. The project was sponsored by Gianfranco Gambigliani, the chief executive officer of ISVOR Fiat, the company's internal training organization. The implementation of the project was supported by Giovanni Testa, director of International Training and Development for ISVOR. The research team consisted of the author and two Italian colleagues: Gino Bonissone and Ivanna Gasperini.

In the early 1970's Fiat was a company on the verge of collapsing. By the late 1980' Fiat was listed by *Fortune* magazine as the second most profitable company in the world (just behind IBM). This dramatic turnaround was largely a function of a number of key leaders in the organization. Many of those leaders, however, were approaching retirement, and it was recognized that their leadership abilities would need to be transferred to, or developed in others, if the company were to continue to be successful.

This modeling project was part of the effort to define the key skills of leadership that had helped to make the company successful, and to design ways to teach and help develop those abilities in others.

Definition of the Project

The project was defined by first establishing both the overall and practical goals of the study, and the presupposition about leadership upon which it would be based. It was then divided into two phases: (1) a Basic Research Phase for initial information gathering, and (2) an Applied Research Phase in which specific leadership skills were explored in more depth, along with the means by which they could be most effectively transferred to others.

Overall Goals

The overall goal of this modeling project was to answer the question, "How it is possible (by means of which methodologies and resources) to improve the leader-collaborator relationship – with the purpose of reaching a higher level of integration (aggregation) of the group?" More precisely, the goal was to determine how to improve managerial effectiveness and skill of middle, divisional and functional managers in relationship to people in their day-to-day interactions. This primarily involved the role/style aspects of leadership in relation to specific objectives.

Scope

The primary scope of the project was to be within what was defined as "micro leadership" by John Nicholls. According to Nicholls (1988) micro leadership, *"focuses on the choice of leadership **style** to create an efficient working atmosphere and obtain willing cooperation in getting the job done by adjusting one's style on the twin dimensions of task and relationship behavior. Choice of leadership style depends on the particular subordinates and the job / task being done, it is, thus, situational and contingent...the leader directs people in organizations in the accomplishment of a specific job or task. If the leadership style is correctly attuned, people perform willingly in an efficient working atmosphere."*

Practical Goals

The practical goals of the research were to define:

1. What excellent leaders do and 'how' they do it - i.e., a description of effective leadership behaviors (interactive tools) and the inner skills (conceptual tools) that sustain those behaviors.

2. How to teach people to acquire the "HOW TOs" with regard to one-to-one relationships and group relationships (if this distinction is a relevant one for the purpose of change).

3. What teaching structure and instruments (seminars, number of modules, time, etc.) will best accomplish the installation of the necessary skills.

Presuppositions

The research was based on the presuppositions that:

1. In defining what effective "leadership" is, it is important to distinguish between (a) a "leader," (b) "leadership" and (c) "leading." The position of "leader" is a role in a particular system. A person in the formal role of a leader may or may not possess leadership skills and be capable of leading. "Leadership" is essentially related to a person's skills, abilities and degree of influence. A good deal of leadership can come from people who are not formal "leaders." "Leading" is the result of using one's role and leadership ability to influence others in some way.

   "Leading" and "leadership" come from the Old English word *lithan*, meaning "to go." According to Merriam-Webster's Dictionary, leadership means "to guide on a way, especially by going in advance." Thus, leadership is often about "going first," and influencing others as much by one's actions as by one's words, as one would lead or guide a dance partner through the steps of a dance. Leadership is also defined as the ability to "direct the operations, activity, or performance of" (as in "leading" an orchestra), and "to bring to some conclusion or condition" (e.g., "lead to believe otherwise").

In its broadest sense, leadership can be defined as the ability to involve others in the process of accomplishing a goal within some larger system or environment. That is, a leader leads or influences a collaborator or group of collaborators towards achieving some end in the context of an organization. In businesses and organizations, 'leadership' is often contrasted with 'management'. Management is typically defined as "getting things done through others." In comparison, leadership is defined as, "getting others to want to do things." Thus, leadership is intimately tied up with motivating and influencing others.

"Management" is usually associated with improving productivity establishing order and stability, and making things run efficiently and smoothly. "Leadership" is required in times of turbulence, social transformation and change.

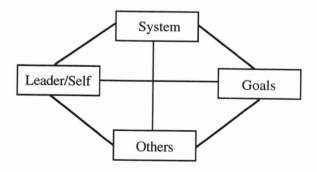

A Leader Involves Others in Reaching Goals Within a System

2. Leadership is a process that is at least partially related to the acquisition of skills. While such abilities as "leadership" are often associated with inborn talent, it was assumed that a skilled manager will perform better than an average manager in adapting to new leadership situations (even if he does not have natural talent). Furthermore, a manager with both talent and skill will outperform one with talent but who has not developed sufficient skills.

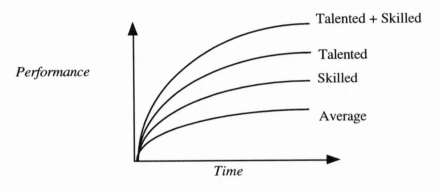

Response To A New Leadership Situation

3. Leadership skills are identifiable and transferable.

4. Behavioral modeling is an effective way to define and transfer practical leadership skills.

Research Phases

The research project was divided into two phases:

1) A Basic Research involving the identification of skills and the creation of a working model of leadership.

2) An Applied Research Phase involving the development of training instruments and programs to seed and transfer incremental micro leadership skills.

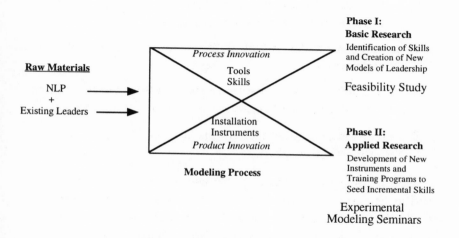

Map of the Overall Research Project

Basic Research Phase

Initial Needs Analysis

An initial needs analysis was conducted that consisted of the following elements:

1. Brief survey of current literature on leadership theories and methods.

2. Observation of video taped formal presentations of Fiat opinion makers.

3. In depth discussions with Italian research team and internal Fiat research coordinators.

4. Interviews with selected top managers in leadership positions at Fiat.

5. Unofficial, informal observations made during negotiation and communication seminars with Fiat top managers.

6. Interviews and discussions made with leaders outside of the Fiat organization.

The focus of this first stage of research was to more clearly define the problem space of the necessary micro leadership skills to be modeled and installed, and to derive a first approximation of which skills and tools would be most valuable and relevant for managers at Fiat.

The conclusions of the general needs analysis were that micro leadership is organized around a cluster of skills which can be divided into the following classifications:

- *Strategic thinking skills* are necessary in order to define and achieve specific goals and objectives. Strategic thinking involves the ability to identify a relevant desired state, assess the starting state and then establish and navigate the appropriate path of transitions states required to reach the desired state. A key element of effective strategic thinking is determining which operators and operations will most efficiently and effectively influence and move the present state in the direction of the desired state.

- *Relational skills* - which have to do with the ability to understand, motivate and communicate with other people. They result in the ability to enter another person's model of the world or perceptual space and get them to recognize problems and objectives and understand the problem space within which they and the company are operating (for example, the ability to shift perceptual positions and recognize meta messages.)

- *Self skills* - which have to do with how the leader deploys himself in a particular situation. Self skills allow the leader to choose or engineer the most appropriate state, attitude, criteria, strategy, etc. with which to enter a situation. In a way, self skills are the processes by which the leader leads himself.

- *Systemic thinking skills* - which are used by the leader to identify and comprehend the problem space in which he, his collaborators and the company is operating. The ability to think systemically in a practical and concrete way is probably the most definitive sign of maturity in a leader. Systemic thinking is at the root of effective strategy formulation and the ability to create functional teams and other systems (for example, ability to recognize multi-level processes and double binds.)

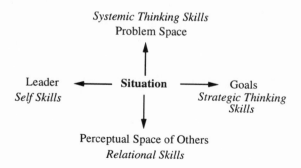

Skill Set of Effective Leadership

Applied Research Phase

Objectives:

The objectives of the applied research phase were to:

1. Identify innovative instruments related to learnable leadership skills (using the process tools of Neuro-Linguistic Programming).

2. Identify ways to incrementally increase the effectiveness of leadership behavior and results in managers through the transfer of specific skills through these instruments.

3. Prepare for the engineering of the end results of the research into a training product which could be disseminated in companies and organizations.

Specific Needs Analysis

Whenever an innovative technology or set of skills is transferred to a new social system (whether it is a physical or behavioral technology) there are key issues and questions that arise in addition to the issue of whether the new skills and technology is effective or needed. This requires a more specific needs analysis involving issues relating to the process of transferring and installing of the new skills and technology, such as:

a. The selection of the most necessary and relevant skills.

b. The selection of the most appropriate and effective tools.

c. The selection of the most effective instructional instruments.

d. The matrixing of skills, tools and instructional instruments.

e. The development of a comprehensive working model to guide the use of skills and tools.

After these more technical issues have been resolved, a learners' analysis needs to be made in order to determine issues such as:

How much?
How big of chunks?
How active?
Kinds of subjects? activities?
How overt?
What beliefs or values are presupposed by the technology? Do they conflict with the existing culture of the social system?

The achievement of these objectives and the analysis of specific needs and learners was done through a set of 'experimental modeling seminars.

Experimental Modeling Seminars

The purpose of the experimental modeling seminars were to extract leadership skills and tools from the behavioral responses and observations of managers through a set of activities designed to elicit both conscious and unconscious competence from effective leaders.

The goals for the modeling seminar were to:

1. Confirm the validity of the general approach of the research.

2. Identify the cognitive and behavioral skills necessary for people in leadership roles to effectively communicate and manage relationships in key leadership situations.

3. Matrix common leadership situations with the appropriate (a) types of skills, (b) NLP tools and (c) teaching instruments required to accomplish effective incremental change in manager's behavior. Coordinate and integrate, as much as possible, the NLP approach to leadership skills with existing leadership training at Fiat - in particular situational leadership (Hersey, Blanchard) and transformational leadership (Bass)

4. Have participating leaders verify and participate in refining relevant distinctions tools and testing/installation instruments.

5. Finalize and refine the instructional instruments to be used for installation in the actual training seminars - i.e., specific scenarios, role plays, questionnaires, etc.

6. Create/confirm the overall rationale for teaching methodology, design principles and instructional instruments.

The modeling process involved the following basic steps.

a. Top managers who had demonstrated good skills as leaders were invited to participate in a three-day seminar as models of effective leadership ability.

b. They participated in a variety of activities involving different kinds of elicitation instruments (discussions, role plays, simulations, etc.). Each day of the seminar focused on a common leadership situation involving the achievement of micro leadership objectives requiring different degrees of task oriented and relational behavior as well as different mixtures of vision and action.

c. The activities and instruments were engineered to draw out specific kinds of skills; conceptual, analytical, observational, procedural, interactive and relational.

d. Each day, the participants were presented with a series of successively more specific approximations of relevant contexts which focused more and more on the interactive and behavioral elements of chosen skill areas. The goal was to minimize the amount/rate of distortion, over-reduction and presuppositions by making the experimental sequence as real and relevant as possible in order to elicit the specific kind of skill we were seeking yet allow for the opportunity to interrupt and elicit cognitive information on the spot.

General Sequence of Modeling/Installation Activities

1) Instrument: **Questionnaires and Discussions**
Scope: General Thinking (related to own role and context)
Skills Accessed: *Conceptual, Relational*

2) Instrument: **Short Scenarios**
Scope: Specific Thinking (distant from own role and context)
Skills Accessed: *Analytical*

3) Instrument: **Role Plays, Demonstrations**
Scope: General Actions (distant from own context)
Skills Accessed: *Procedural, Observational*

4) Instrument: **Simulations, "Fish Bowl"**
Scope: Specific Actions (close to own role and context)
Skills Accessed: *Interactive, Observational*

e. The instruments and contexts were designed in such a way that they could be used for installation tools as well as elicitation tools. Thus, in the zero base seminar, these activities will serve as both diagnostic and instructional instruments for the seeding of incremental skills.

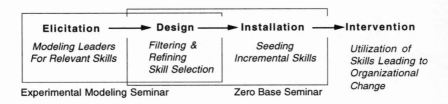

Sequence of Modeling Activities

f. The activities were video taped for further observation by the research team. Within the context of the seminar, participating leaders themselves took part in some ongoing modeling of both verbal and non-verbal skills under the guidance of the research team.

g. In addition to fine tuning the elicitation methods to be used for the larger research effort, the experimental seminars provided an opportunity to more completely and practically select and matrix the types of tools most relevant for leadership with types of skills and elicitation/installation instruments that most effectively address those skills. These tools fell into several categories:

1) Conceptual Tools

2) Analytical Tools

3) Procedural Tools

4) Instructional Tools

Selection of Contexts and Examples

While the overall emphasis of the modeling was on transcontextual skills, it was necessary and important to select specific types of situations in which those skills were to be applied. Three situations were chosen: 1) problem solving, 2) delegation and 3) training on the job. These three different situations were selected because they covered the span of situations a leader is most likely to find himself in and focus the mix of skills, tools and instructional instruments that are required for effective leadership performance.

The three situations also formed a logical dependency or sequence of skills:

1. *Problem solving* is a more or less a symmetrical activity and covers the most basic skills for any goal oriented behavior. A general definition of a problem is "any situation where the present state does not match the desired state". Given this definition, problem solving is usually at the core of most interpersonal relations and communication interactions. Even delegation and job training issues usually revolve around the solving of some sort of problem - i.e., to move the present state more toward some desired state.

2. *Delegation* is clearly a complementary process. In fact, delegation may be defined as a social contract to solve a problem together within the framework of complementary roles. It involves problem solving abilities but also has a much more relational emphasis.

3. *Training on the job* is what would be called a "meta-complementary" activity - one in which the leader is not in a direct management role but is leading at a more abstracted or 'meta' level. Training on the job has been defined as a process of 'permanent education'. It involves the way in which someone solves problems and delegates within a given role, social system and context.

The problem space of each situation successively widens to incorporate the elements of the previous situation but adds new variables to be contended with.

Day 1	Day 2	Day 3
Problem Solving	Delegation	Training on the Job
High Task	Task and Relationship	High Relationship
High Vision	Vision and Action	High Action

**Contexts to be Studied During
The Experimental Modeling Seminar**

Sequence of Modeling Activities

The modeling activities took place in the following sequence:

1. The first activity involved the participating managers filling out questionnaires relating to how they handled particular situations (problem solving, delegation or training on the job), exploring both one-to-one interactions and interactions with a group.

    The questionnaire was designed to elicit information in the form of a T.O.T.E. – i.e., the goals, evidence procedures and operations used by the managers to accomplish micro leadership objectives in the situation. The questionnaires also helped to define common contexts at Fiat relating to the chosen leadership situation.

    The purpose of the questionnaires was to elicit and encourage general thinking about the situation so that the problem space of the situation could be defined and shared by all of the participants. The questionnaire also provided a reference experience with which the participant's could begin to think of their behaviors in terms of the T.O.T.E. distinctions.

After the questionnaires had been completed there was a full group discussion of the answers. The responses were tabulated on flip charts and used to identify general patterns of responses. Typologies of responses were used to identify and explore different levels of patterns and their relevance to leadership and leadership styles. Also, since this was a modeling seminar, the results of these questionnaires were used for diagnostic purposes for the design of seminars to install leadership capabilities.

2. Following the discussion of the questionnaire, a brief scenario defining a common context for the chosen type of leadership situation was distributed to the group members for discussion in small groups. Again, the results of the discussions were elicited and tabulated with the full group. During the full group discussion of the results potentially relevant distinctions were introduced to the group and evaluated as to their significance and practicality.

3. Following the scenarios, participants enacted a set of role plays relating to the context of the scenario constructed on the basis of themes and patterns derived from the tabulations of discussion results. The role plays were conducted in a 'fish bowl' style, first with the whole group as observers and then breaking into smaller experimental groups. The role plays were run such that there was the option to substitute group members into the leadership role so that differences and similarities between styles, skills and use of tools could be identified and compared.

The role plays were organized to include lateral and one-to-few relationships as well as one-to-one vertical relations depending upon the issues that came up during the discussions.

Observations of specific behavioral and cognitive patterns were made explicitly during the role plays as well as any patterns relating to specific problem solving tools such as Well-formedness conditions for Outcomes or the 'As If' frame, etc.

4. Finally, the participants were asked to create simulations that were less restricted and more relevant to their own personal contexts to allow for more personal involvement and spontaneity. The simulations were conducted in small groups in a 'fish bowl' framework and, again, effective behaviors, skills and tools were explicitly commented upon by members of the research team.

Instruments	Skills	Tools
Questionnaire Discussion	Conceptual	T.O.T.E. Model
Scenarios/Cases Discussion	Analytical	S.C.O.R.E. Model
Role Plays Demonstrations - experimentation inside the context of the Role Plays	Procedural Observational	'As if' Frame Calibration Pacing and Leading
Simulations Supervision ('Fish Bowl')	Interactive Relational	Meta Programs Levels Perceptual Positions

**General Areas Covered by the
Sequence of Modeling Activities**

The Zero Base Seminar

A zero base seminar was constructed on the basis of the experimental seminar and conducted in March of 1990. The general sequence of situations (problem solving - delegation - training on the job) were maintained in order to verify and refine the general approach. The instructional instruments (questionnaire, scenario, role play, simulation) was also preserved and adapted to fit a non-experimental training based on those made up by the experimental group participants. The basic NLP models of SOAR, SCORE, TOTE and Communication Matrix were the essential theoretical and behavioral framework presented in the seminar.

Follow up Seminar.

A follow up seminar was designed and made available to participants of both the experimental seminar and zero base participants in May of 1990. The purpose of the follow up seminar was to test and reinforce the skills developed in the previous leadership seminars and further prepare for the general engineering of a wider program involving NLP to develop communication and relational skills.

The specific results of this sequence of seminars are summarized in detail in the following chapters of this book.

Chapter 6

Problem Solving

Overview of Chapter 6

- **Modeling Leadership Skills in Problem Solving**
- **Information Gathering Methodology**
- **Patterns and Results**
  - **Types of Problems in Groups and Organizations**
  - **Defining Problem Space and Solutions Space**
  - **General Problem Solving Cycle**
  - **Punctuating Key Elements of a Problem Space**
    - **The S.C.O.R.E. Model**
  - **Operational Approaches to Problem Solving**
- **Applications and Tools**
  - **Defining a S.C.O.R.E**
  - **Eliciting Multiple S.C.O.R.E.s**
  - **Interactive Skills of Problem Solving**
  - **Managing the Creative Process of a Group**
  - **'Imagineering' Group Process**

Modeling Leadership Skills in Problem Solving

One of the most common situations requiring leadership is that of problem solving. Problem Solving can be classified as a "complex cognitive" skill, which is supported by certain interactive ("complex behavioral") and linguistic skills. The goal of this part of the leadership research study was to define the way that leaders: (1) mentally organized and thought about common organizational problems, and (2) approached involving a group in the identification of problem elements, and in finding and implementing potential solutions.

Information Gathering Methodology

The modeling was done in a "co-modeling" framework, involving the three members of the research team. This was to ensure a "triple description" of all identified patterns. It also allowed different members to focus on different distinctions (cognitive, linguistic or behavioral) at various times.

The modeling activities were designed to determine which NLP distinctions and features were most relevant for effective leadership in problem solving in terms of the following criteria:

a. The degree to which the distinctions enriched the overall performance of both effective and novice leaders.

b. The intuitive fit of the distinctions (code congruency) with the way in which leaders naturally perceive situations.

c. The degree to which the distinctions added something new which 'releases' unconscious competence.

The sequence of modeling activities was structured in order to move from focusing on the cognitive skills at the basis of problem solving to the more interactive aspects of involving a group in the problem solving process. The modeling activities took place in the following order:

Initial Questionnaire

For the first activity, the participating managers filled out questionnaires relating to how they handled particular problem solving situations, working in the context of a group or team. The questionnaire was designed to elicit information in the form of a T.O.T.E. - i.e., the goals, evidence procedures and operations used by the managers to both leading others and finding potential solutions with respect to common organizational problems. The purpose of the questionnaires was to elicit and encourage general thinking about the situation so that common patterns could be defined and shared by all of the participants.

The questionnaire was worded as follows:

T.O.T.E. Questionnaire for Leadership Skills in Problem Solving

1. Write a brief description of a typical example of a problem solving situation, involving a group of others, in which you must use "leadership" ability in the context of your role in the company.

2. When you are in this kind of context and situation, what are the goals or objectives that guide your actions? (List them in short sentences or key words.)

3. What do you typically use as evidence to know you are accomplishing those goals?

4. What do you typically do to get to the goal - what are some specific steps and activities that you use to achieve your problem solving goals in that context?

5. When you experience unexpected problems or difficulties in achieving your goals in this context, what specific activities or steps do you take?

6. Which, if any, of these problem solving goals, evidence procedures or activities would change if the context of the problem solving situation changed to a one-to-one interaction? How, specifically, would they change?

After the questionnaires had been completed, there was a full group discussion of the answers. The responses were tabulated on flip charts and used to identify general patterns of responses. Typologies of responses were used to identify and explore different levels of patterns and their relevance to leadership and problem solving.

Written Scenario

Following the discussion of the questionnaire, a brief scenario defining a common context requiring leadership skills in problem solving was distributed to the group members for discussion in small groups. The specific scenario given for discussion was:

You are the person in charge of factory "B". The chief of your maintenance Department manages 6 eight-man teams, working under 6 foremen. You are worried because these teams don't work efficiently. As a matter of fact, the workers in the teams tend to do just what strictly concerns their specific tasks. As a result, work and programs of this Department are slowed down. Only in cases of emergency is this routine overcome. You also know, on the other hand, that the capabilities and competence of the workers are higher and allow for more effective utilization.

How would you deal with this problem?

Again, the results of the discussions were elicited and tabulated with the full group. During the full group discussion of the results potentially relevant distinctions were introduced to the group and evaluated as to their significance and practicality.

Role Plays and Simulations

Following the scenarios, participants enacted role plays, which were based on the scenario and constructed as a result of the themes and patterns derived from the tabulations of discussion results. Participants were also asked to create simulations that were less restricted and more relevant to their own personal contexts to allow for more personal involvement and spontaneity. The role plays and simulations were conducted in a 'fish bowl' style, first with the whole group as observers and then breaking into smaller experimental groups. The role plays were run such that there was the option to substitute group members into the leadership role so that differences and similarities between styles, skills and use of tools could be identified and compared.

The role plays were organized to include lateral and one-to-few relationships as well as one-to-one vertical relations depending upon the issues that came up during the discussions.

The following is an example of a role play/simulation that was used to explore some of the interactive and relational leadership skills (as well as the cognitive and linguistic skills) associated with effective problem solving:

Roles:
1. Personnel Manager
2. Marketing Manager
3. Production Manager
4. Project Leader

Context:

The Project Leader must organize a team to design a product for an expanding market - for example, to design a car to be introduced into Eastern Europe. The project leader has no technical competence in the product area. The policy problems have already been solved. The task of the project leader is to coordinate the various specializations to achieve the goal but be aware of real problems.

Observations of specific behavioral and cognitive patterns were made explicitly by the members of the research team during the role plays, as well as any patterns relating to specific NLP problem solving tools, such as "Well-formedness conditions for Outcomes" or the "'As If' frame," etc.

As a method to insure the "code congruency" of various NLP distinctions, the participating managers were also asked to make comments on their observations, from the perspective of either being in the role play or as an observer. As the NLP distinctions were introduced, the research team members noted which ones seemed to be picked up and incorporated naturally into the comments of the mangers, and which ones seemed to "fade into the background." For example, terms which were picked up and incorporated immediately by the participating managers included distinctions such as:

"problem space"
"levels of change" (i.e., "environment," "behavior," "capabilities," "beliefs," "values," "identity" - "where," "when," "what," "how," "why," "who")
the S.C.O.R.E. Model distinctions ("symptom," "cause," "outcome," "resources," "effect"),
"perceptual positions"
"dreamer, realist and critic"

Other terms, such as, "accessing cues," "submodalities," and "anchoring," seemed more foreign, and even confusing, to the managers' way of thinking and organizing their experience; even though the other NLP terms were just as new to the managers.

Modeling Filters

In order to identify the most relevant skills and tools used by the leaders, the research group members applied the following filters to their observations of the participating leaders as they completed each modeling activity:

1. Which distinctions were consistently demonstrated at the level of unconscious competence, as evidenced by the leader's actions, language patterns and responses?

2. Which distinctions were immediately activated at the level of conscious competence, as evidenced by observa-

tions of the seminar participants from observer position in the 'fish bowl' activities? The "code congruency" of the distinctions was also checked by asking the participants:

a. Are these effective/relevant distinctions to describe, release, learn, or transfer the skills of leadership?
b. Is this an effective instrument to get at the essence of leadership?
c. Does it "fit" - i.e., draw out or illuminate a structure that expands or enriches your leadership capabilities?

Those distinctions which arose as patterns of unconscious competence but were not activated through the NLP labels, were to become an engineering problem for the Zero Base seminar. It may have been that they were biased (negatively) in terms of intuitive fit by the mode of presentation or by the specific type of situation.

3. Which distinctions helped to fill in "missing links" that helped to 'release' natural abilities or move between different levels of activities? (There is always competence at some level of specificity.)

Patterns and Results

The following is a synthesis of the key patterns, distinctions and processes that emerged from the various activities relating to leadership and problem solving.

Types of Problems in Groups and Organizations

There is an important general distinction between recurrent problems and 'virgin' problems in organizational problem solving. These different types of problems involve fundamentally different types of problem spaces, and need to be approached differently in order to be appropriately resolved.

Recurrent problems are those encountered during the execution of standard procedures employed to achieve specific company results (e.g., problems of "quality" or "efficiency"). 'Recurrent' problems may be further divided into: (a) problems in overall approach, versus (b) mistakes or variances in specific procedures.

The effects of such problems on company results may be divided into those which are: (1) measurable or quantitative and can be 'chunked' into a number of pieces, versus those which are (2) not measurable and are more qualitative; such as quality of service.

Effectively resolving 'recurring' problems involves careful analysis in order to pinpoint the cause of the problem so that it may be appropriately corrected or adjusted. Leadership with respect to this type of problem requires the ability to "narrow" the problem space, and identify the specific individuals and measures that are necessary to clarify the source of the problem and implement the most effective solution.

'Virgin' problems are those which have no precedent in the company and are associated with a high degree of uncertainty in relation to both procedures and results (such as designing a new product for an expanding market). 'Virgin' problems tend to be precipitated by changes in the environment or organizational system. To successfully deal with this type of problem, the leader needs to gather together the appropriate number of perspectives and overcome the uncertainties by creating a shared understanding of the problem.

In 'virgin' problems, many aspects of the problem space are uncertain or volatile because the problem is either new or there is a big change in some dimension of the broader system such as the market, the political climate, etc. 'Virgin' problems involve a greater degree of uncertainty and require a greater need for interaction, communication and a shared understanding of the problem space among the individuals addressing the problem. Recurring problems generally involve less complexity and smaller increments of change or adjustment.

Thus, there are different kinds of group evidences and operations required to effectively approach these different types of problems. Evidences for the resolution of recurrent problems are generally defined in terms of specific outcomes to be achieved in successive times and stages. Evidences for 'virgin' problems are generally defined in terms of the level of consensus and integration of different individuals and perspectives in the successive stages.

Recurring problems generally require operations relating to the breakdown of problem elements and the delegation of specific actions. 'Virgin' problems generally require operations relating to forming a team, synthesizing information about problem elements and generating new perspectives and multiple descriptions of the problem space.

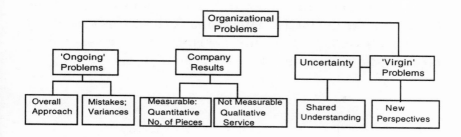

There are Two General Types of Problems Leaders Must Address in Organizations: 'Recurrent' Problems and 'Virgin' Problems

Leadership is involved in different ways in the two types of situations, but is especially relevant with respect to new problems in highly uncertain situations. Since addressing 'virgin' problems involves dealing with uncertainty, the goals and evidences tend to revolve around creating shared understandings and consensus involved in defining problems, determining outcomes, and sharing common competence and knowledge. On the one hand, the group is sharing experiences and understandings. On the other hand, the group is attempting to generate new perspectives, draw out individual strengths and utilize individual competence.

The degree and the type of interaction necessary to address a 'virgin' problem is more intense than in the typical approach for dealing with recurrent problems. This introduces special relational issues related to communicating and responding to members of the group because of the complexity of interactions.

'Recurrent' or 'ongoing' institutional problems tend to be more linear and structured. Operations primarily consist of 'chunking' and analyzing the problem into its components and delegating responsibilities to the appropriate functions. Evidence procedures relate to the completion of specific steps, timing and deadlines.

'Virgin' problems are more systemic in nature. Operations involve a more interactive, lateral approach such as partnering or team building. Evidence for progress is measured in terms of the consensus of the group.

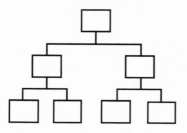

Appropriate Structure for
Dealing with 'Ongoing' Problems
Related to Specific Company Results.

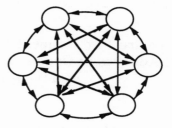

Appropriate Structure for
Dealing with 'Virgin' Problems
Related to Change and Uncertainty.

Different Types of Problem Solving Strategies and Leadership Skills Are Required for Dealing With 'Virgin' Problems than for 'Recurrent' Problems

Defining Problem Space and Solution Space

A key element of effective problem-solving for problems of any type is defining the 'problem space.' Problem space is not just the physical space associated with a problem. Relationships, values, perceptions and beliefs might all contribute to the problem space. The problem space is defined by the elements, both physical and non-physical which create or contribute to the problem.

In order to solve a problem it is necessary to find a 'solution space.' A solution space contains alternatives and resources that allow us to either overcome, transform or avoid the problem. If, however, the alternatives and resources available in the solution space are not enough to address all of the elements of the problem space, an insufficient solution will arise. The solution space needs to be broader than the problem space. It is possible to find inadequate solutions because they don't address all of the elements of the problem.

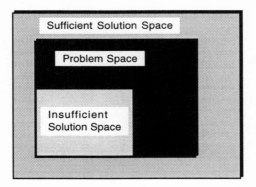

The 'Solution Space' Must be Wider than the 'Problem Space' in Order to Produce an Effective Solution

Some essential cognitive and interactive skills are required to help widen the available solution space; and also to uncover and define the problem space to begin with. Thus, effective problem solving involves two stages: 1) to enrich and clarify our perception of the problem space and 2) to define or create some area of solution space that is broad enough to address all of the relevant aspects of the problem space.

Before we can find a solution, we have to first comprehend the variables that are creating the problem space. The basic principle of finding 'solution space' is that you can't solve the problem with the same kind of thinking or the same map that is, in fact, creating the problem. In the words of Albert Einstein, "Our thinking creates problems that the same thinking can't solve." A map that leads us into a problem space may not show us the way out.

The whole goal in effective problem solving is to find a way of thinking that is not the same thinking that is creating the problem. Then, hopefully, this other way of thinking will lead to a solution space, that is at least as broad or broader than the problem space, in which the appropriate alternatives and resources can be found.

General Problem Solving Cycle

The process of defining 'problem space' and 'solution space' involves a general cycle of information gathering and implementation that reflects two core criteria of effective leadership in problem solving. The most effective solutions will be those which most 'thoroughly' cover the 'relevant' elements within the system which are contributing to the problem. Thus, effective problem solving must maintain a balance between thoroughness and relevance.

Thoroughness involves checking all of the possible contributing factors to a particular problem or goal. *Relevance* involves defining those factors which are most significant in the production of the problem or the achievement of the goal; or which provide the most leverage in influencing the present state of the problem. Thus, there is a continual cycling in the process of problem solving between 1) thoroughly identifying problem factors and potential elements of the problem space, and 2) determining which of those factors and elements are most relevant in terms of producing, and therefore, solving the problem.

Relevant information is found through the process of the stages of:

a. Gathering information about the problem and problem space.

b. Filtering the information in order to select the relevant factors and leverage points.

c. Applying the information that has been gathered and filtered in the implementation of a plan or solution.

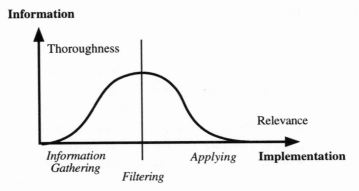

Information

Thoroughness

Relevance

Information Gathering   *Applying*   **Implementation**

Filtering

Problem Solving Cycle

Typically, problems are not solved in a single cycle but rather through a series of successive approximations; in which multiple iterations of the problem solving cycle converge upon the most effective solution. After information has been gathered, filtered and applied, the results of that cycle are evaluated and the next cycle is applied to those results. More information is gathered, then filtered and applied. This series of successive approximations may be characterized by a path of 'Elaboration-Decision' cycles. In the 'elaboration' phase of the cycle, knowledge is gathered in order to exhaustively check all potentially significant factors. In the 'decision' phase of the cycle, information is filtered for relevance and applied in order to move to the next step or transition state in the path to the eventual solution.

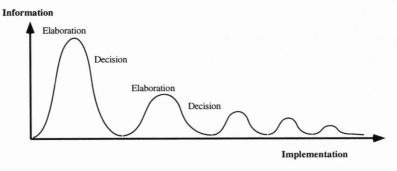

Information

Elaboration

Decision

Elaboration

Decision

Implementation

Sequence of 'Elaboration/Decision' Cycles

Punctuating Key Elements of a Problem Space – The S.C.O.R.E. Model

A *problem* can essentially be defined as the *gap* between your present state and your desired state, and the issues that have to be dealt with in order to get to the desired state.

The *S.C.O.R.E. Model* (Dilts & Epstein, 1987, 1991) is a useful problem solving model that identifies the primary components necessary for effectively organizing information about the problem space related to a particular goal or process of change. The letters stand for *Symptoms, Causes, Outcome, Resources,* and *Effects.* These elements represent the minimum amount of information that needs to be gathered to effectively address that problem space.

In the process of moving toward a desired state, for instance, symptoms come up in the form of constraints, resistances and interferences to reaching the outcome. Symptoms are typically the most obvious aspect of a problem. A typical kind of *symptom* in a company might be a drop in profits or productivity.

Of course, effective problem solving involves finding and treating the cause of a particular symptom or set of symptoms. *Causes* are often less obvious, broader and more systemic in nature than the particular symptom that is being manifested at the moment. A drop in profit or productivity may be the result of something related to competition, organization, leadership, change in the market, change in technology, communications channels, or something else. What you identify as the cause determines where you will seek to create the solution.

The desired *effect* of achieving a particular goal or outcome can also a be significant factor in defining a problem space. A specific *outcome* is generally a step along a path to longer range effects. It is important that the solution to a problem is congruent to the longer range desired effects. Sometimes the way in which an outcome is reached can actually interfere with reaching the longer term target; i.e., it is possible to "win the battle but lose the war."

Thus, a problem space is defined by the relationship between the goal or outcome, the kind of symptoms that are getting in the way of achieving the outcome, the causes of those symptoms and the longer range desired effects of reaching the outcome. In order to find the *resources* that will produce an effective solution for a particular symptom, it is necessary to know the causes of the symptom, the outcome and the ultimate desired effect to be reached.

Leadership skills may be required in defining any element of the S.C.O.R.E. space. In addition to finding potential resources and alternatives, leadership may be required in order to establish outcomes, anticipate effects, define and measure symptoms and uncover causes.

In defining these elements of the problem and solution spaces, it may be necessary to 1) cluster information into larger or smaller 'chunks', 2) focus on different aspects of the problem space, 3) take different perspectives and perceptual positions and 4) create multiple descriptions of the problem and potential solutions.

Leadership skills have applications in different areas of problem-solving – not all of which will produce solutions, but which may be required to get to a solution. Depending upon how specific or general a problem situation is, the process of 'problem solving' might produce an immediate result or it might only produce steps to results. Some solutions may require an intensive amount of problem solving effort applied over a space of months or years. The process of defining symptoms, outcomes, causes and potential effects is an ongoing process.

Operational Approaches to Problem Solving

There are several different general approaches to problem solving depending upon what is known and what is uncertain within a particular 'problem space'.

When there is relatively complete information on a general level, operational problem solving proceeds by beginning with an overall problem statement, and then breaking it into its component pieces and elements in order to define potential resources and solution areas.

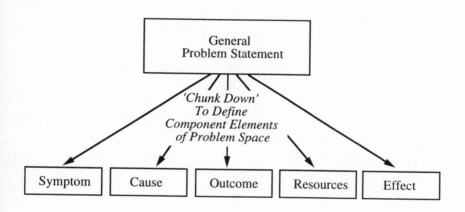

Path 1: 'Chunking Down' A General Problem Statement Into Its Component Elements

When the general understanding of the problem is incomplete or uncertain, operational problem solving proceeds by collecting whatever is known about the component pieces and elements of the 'problem space' and then synthesizing those elements into a general understanding and statement of the overall problem.

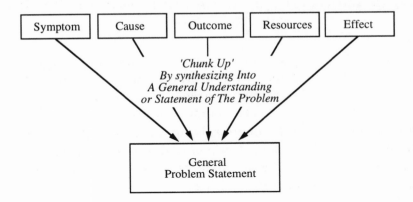

Path 2: 'Chunking Up' Specific Problem Elements Into A General Understanding Of The Problem Space

When both the general understanding of the problem is incomplete or uncertain *and* the knowledge of the individual elements making up the problem is also incomplete, operational problem solving proceeds by focusing on what is most certain and 'elaborating' or branching to make approximations or guesses about the other component pieces and elements of the 'problem space'.

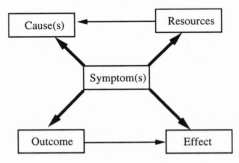

'Elaboration' of Other Problem Space
Elements From the Symptom(s)

Path 3: Elaborating From One Element of a Problem Space to Define Other Relevant Elements

Applications and Tools

The remainder of this section contains a number of tools and strategies, that can be used in practical problem solving situations, which were derived from the modeling study described in this chapter.

Defining a S.C.O.R.E.

The cognitive skills of problem solving involve the ability to define the 'problem space' of the situation, and identify potential areas of 'solution space', by establishing the relationship between the elements defined by the S.C.O.R.E Model:

a. *Symptoms* - typically the most noticeable and conscious aspects of a present problem or problem state; such as confusions or conflicts in relation to changes in policies or procedures.

b. *Causes* - the underlying elements responsible for creating and maintaining the symptoms; such as rigid or outdated cognitive maps or limiting beliefs and assumptions ('thought viruses') that lead to the conflict or confusion.

c. *Outcomes* - the particular goals or desired states that would take the place of the symptoms; such as the acceptance and implementation of the new policies or procedures.

d. *Resources* - the underlying elements responsible for removing the causes of the symptoms and for manifesting and maintaining the desired outcomes; such as tools and alternatives for communicating and clarifying the where, when, what, how, why and who of the change in policies or procedures.

e. *Effects* - the longer term results of achieving a particular outcome; such as the improvement in productivity, profitability or quality of working environment anticipated as a result of the change of policies or procedures.

'Problem Space' Questions

Fill in the answers to the questions below to define the basic 'problem space' of a problem or situation you are attempting to resolve.

1. What is the *'symptom'* in this problem?

2. What is the *'cause'* of the symptom in this problem?

3. What is the desired *'outcome'* or goal of this problem?

4. What would be the longer term *'effect'* of reaching that goal?

5. What *'resource'* would help address the cause?

6. What *'resource'* would help achieve the outcome?

Eliciting Multiple S.C.O.R.E.s

Complex, systemic problems often manifest themselves in terms of more than one symptom; and any particular symptom may have multiple causes. Both projects and problems may involve several different desired outcomes and effects. In gathering information about a particular problem or 'problem space', it is often necessary to identify and synthesize multiple symptoms, outcomes, etc.

For instance, in a complex organization, the problem may present different symptoms to different parts of the organization. That is, the symptoms of a 'quality' problem may show up in terms of "increased costs" to a production manager, but in terms of "reduced sales" to a marketing manager. Effective problem solving in an organization involves the recognition of such symptoms and their interrelationships. Sometimes, in order to successfully diagnose a problem, its causes and potential solutions, it is necessary to look at the relationship between several symptoms.

Another issue with respect to a complex problem or problem space relates to the 'level' at which the symptom, cause, outcome, etc. are occurring. For instance, a symptom may be at the level of 'behavior', such as a decrease in performance or productivity. The cause of such a symptom, however, may be at some other level. There may be environmental influences, for example, that interfere with the performance. The cause, however, could also be due to a motivational interference coming from the level of beliefs and values; or from a lack of capabilities such as communication skills or leadership skills.

Thus, it can also be necessary to seek symptoms, causes and outcomes, etc., at different levels of process in order to effectively define the whole problem space.

The following pages provide an instrument with which multiple perspectives relating to a particular problem space may be identified and synthesized. By presenting the S.C.O.R.E. questions, listed on the previous page, to a number of different individuals, it is possible to gather a variety of different views of the elements which make up a particular problem. These answers then need to be synthesized in different ways in order to make sense of the information and coordinate a plan or solution.

The instrument provides spaces for multiple responses relating to the various S.C.O.R.E. distinctions to be gathered together. The different perspectives of the problem space may be summarized or organized according to the function or role of the individual who is answering the questions. This supports the ability to see how a similar problem may appear differently to people in different parts of a system.

Problem State Summary

Use the spaces below to summarize and relate different perspectives of symptoms and causes associated with the problem space.

Team Member #1: _____

Symptoms   **Causes**

_____   _____

_____   _____

Team Member #2: _____

Symptoms   **Causes**

_____   _____

_____   _____

Team Member #3: _____

Symptoms   **Causes**

_____   _____

_____   _____

Team Member #4: _____

Symptoms   **Causes**

_____   _____

_____   _____

Desired State Summary

Use the spaces below to summarize and relate different perspectives of outcomes and effects associated with the problem space.

Team Member #1: _____
Outcomes   **Effects**

_____   _____

_____   _____

Team Member #2: _____
Outcomes   **Effects**

_____   _____

_____   _____

Team Member #3: _____
Outcomes   **Effects**

_____   _____

_____   _____

Team Member #4: _____
Outcomes   **Effects**

_____   _____

_____   _____

Resource Summary

Use the spaces below to summarize and relate different perspectives of resources related to the problem space.

Resources for Addressing Symptoms	**Resources for Addressing Causes**

Team Member #1: _____

_____   _____

Team Member #2: _____

_____   _____

Team Member #3: _____

_____   _____

Team Member #4: _____

_____   _____

Resources for Achieving the Desired Outcome and Effect

Team Member #1: _____

_____   _____

Team Member #2: _____

_____   _____

Team Member #3: _____

_____   _____

Team Member #4: _____

_____   _____

Illustration of the Multiple S.C.O.R.E.

As an illustration of how the instrument might be used, consider the following scenario.

TransTech is a young innovative company which produces a revolutionary hand-held language translator. A user may speak English in one side of the translator and it will translate the words into another language and play out the translation to the listener. Likewise the listener may speak in his own language and the TransTech unit will translate it into English. Demand for the TransTech translator has grown tremendously. As sales have increased, however, quality problems have begun to arise. There are an increasing number of customer complaints relating to malfunctions in the translator unit and sales have begun to drop off. Competitors have begun to make imitations of the TransTech translator and there is a growing concern about losing market share.

You are a manager who has been given the assignment of being the project leader of a team whose task is to come up with some suggestions for how to address this problem. You have no previous history with the project and no technical background with this type of device. You will be interacting with four functional heads of the division: Marketing, Engineering, Production and Finance.

The following pages provide an example of how the Multiple S.C.O.R.E. worksheets might be filled out by the project leader, after having submitted the basic 'Problem Space' (S.C.O.R.E.) questions to the various functional heads.

Problem State Summary

Use the spaces below to summarize and relate different perspectives of symptoms and causes associated with the problem space.

Team Member #1: Marketing

Symptoms	**Causes**
Unhappy customers	Product malfunctions
Reduced sales	Lack of confidence in product
Lower market share	Increased number of competitors

Team Member #2: Production

Symptoms	**Causes**
Increase in product defects	Inadequate resources
Inability to keep up with demand	High growth rate of market

Team Member #3: Engineering

Symptoms	**Causes**
Reduction in innovation	Dealing with problems of current product
Improved competitor imitations	Not enough emphasis on security and protection

Team Member #4: Finance

Symptoms	**Causes**
Drop in profits	Reduced sales and increased returns
Cash flow problems	Decrease in short term income and increase in longer term expenditures

Desired State Summary

Use the spaces below to summarize and relate different perspectives of outcomes and effects associated with the problem space.

Team Member #1: Marketing

Outcomes

Satisfied customers
Stabilize/Increase sales
Maintain market position

Effects

Strong customer base
Survival and growth
Stay competitive

Team Member #2: Production

Outcomes

More fully functioning units
Increased production capacity

Effects

Satisfaction and pride
Reduction of pressure and stress

Team Member #3: Engineering

Outcomes

Appropriate innovation rate
Superior product design

Effects

Stay flexible and competitive
Continue reputation as
industry leader

Team Member #4: Finance

Outcomes

Increased revenue
Balanced budget

Effects

Maintain viability
Fulfill commitments

Resource Summary

Use the spaces below to summarize and relate different perspectives of resources related to the problem space.

Resources for Addressing Symptoms	Resources for Addressing Causes
Team Member #1: Marketing	
Increased customer relations	Customer feedback and involvement
Team Member #2: Production	
'Re-engineering' of production process	Subcontractors
Team Member #3: Engineering	
Refocusing of design effort	Strengthening of team motivation and leadership
Team Member #4: Finance	
Find a new area of immediate sales potential	Partnerships with suppliers

Resources for Achieving the Desired Outcome and Effect

Team Member #1: Marketing	
Open untapped market areas	Model effective competitors
Team Member #2: Production	
Strengthen alliances	Find interim help
Team Member #3: Engineering	
Re-establish a clear vision	Improve team process
Team Member #4: Finance	
Update plan and budget	An accurate model of the market

Interactive Skills of Problem Solving

The greatest need for leadership in problem solving arises in situations of change and transition. In addition to the cognitive process of working with the distinctions of the S.C.O.R.E. model, interactive leadership skills may be required to help people either (1) recognize the need for change, or (2) manage resistances to change.   This is especially important in 'virgin' situations.

The managers participating in the leadership study, for instance, felt that the simulation involving the design of a new product for an expanding market represented a fundamental and increasingly common situation.   They felt that managers are often placed in situations in which they must lead others in projects in which they, as the leader, lack specific technical skills with respect to the project they are managing.   The solution revolves around the leader deciding (a) where to focus attention, and (b) what kind of attitude or inner state to take on in relation to the roles and personalities of the other team members, and with respect to the problem space in general.

If a key technical person is not optimistic for example, the project leader may take "a more active attitude" and focus on setting steps and timing with respect to the project. The leaders in the modeling study often talked about the need to be "optimistic," "realistic," or "critical" at various times, depending on which they felt was appropriate for the particular group they were leading.   These distinctions reflect a fundamental typology of states and attitudes used by many effective leaders.

For instance, somebody once said of Walt Disney, *"...there were actually three different Walts: the **dreamer**, the **realist**, and the **spoiler**. You never knew which one was coming into your meeting."* This is not only an insight into Disney but also into the process of creativity and problem solving – a process that Disney called "imagineering."   Imagineering involves the coordination of these three subprocesses: Dreamer, Realist and Critic, all of which are necessary to identify effective solutions.

A Dreamer without a Realist cannot turn ideas into tangible expressions. A Critic and a Dreamer without a realist just become stuck in a perpetual conflict. A Dreamer and a Realist might create things, but they might not be very good ideas without a Critic. The Critic helps to evaluate and refine the products of creativity (when destructive, a Critic is a "spoiler;" when constructive, a Critic is an "advisor"). There is a humorous example of a manager who prided himself on his innovative thinking abilities but lacked some of the Realist and Critic perspective. The people who worked in the company used to say, "He has an idea a minute...and some of them are good."

Effective problem solving involves a synthesis of these different processes or phases. The Dreamer is necessary in order to form new ideas and goals. The Realist is necessary as a means to transform ideas into concrete expressions. The Critic is necessary as a filter for refining ideas and avoiding possible problems.

Managing the Creative Process of a Group

Disney's creative process can also be applied to groups and teams. The creative cycle of a group or team often involves the natural movement between 'dreamer' (the big picture or 'vision'), 'realist' (the establishment of micro objectives to reach the larger goal), and 'critic' (the search for missing links and potential problems).

"Balance" is a core criterion expressed by many leaders as being key in managing the creative process of a group. In order to effectively solve a problem or produce a plan, no one stage or thinking style can be favored at the expense of the others. The various thinking styles encompassed by 'Dreamer', 'Realist' and 'Critic' apply differently in achieving and implementing ideas, and in solving problems:

The Dreamer helps to generate alternatives and possibilities.
The Realist helps to define actions.
The Critic helps to evaluate payoffs and drawbacks.

Thus, for effective group problem solving it is important to incorporate:

1. All three of the stages of the creative cycle (Dreamer, Realist, Critic)

2. The different points of view of the group members in all three stages.

A key part of managing a group's creativity involves the ability to direct the group or team members into the specific cognitive and interactive processes required to implement or fulfill this cycle. Managing the creative process of a group involves establishing physical and psychological constraints which direct the group's process in relation to the phase of the creative cycle they are in.

Disney, for example, had different rooms for the dreamer, realist and critic. He had one room that was a dreamer room which had pictures and inspirational drawings and sayings all over the walls. Everything was chaotic and colorful in this room, and criticisms were not allowed—only dreams! For their realist space, the animators had their own drawing tables, stocked with all kinds of modern equipment, tools and instruments that they would need to manifest the dreams. The tables were arranged in a large room in which all of the animators could see and talk to other animators. For the critic, Disney had a little room that was underneath the stairs where they would look at the prototype pencil sketches and evaluate them. The room always seemed cramped and hot, so they called it the 'sweatbox.'

The following is a summary of the basic cognitive and physical patterns associated with each of these key thinking styles.

Dreamer

The Dreamer phase of a process is oriented towards the longer term future. It involves thinking in terms of the bigger picture and the larger chunks in order to generate new alternatives and choices. The emphasis of the Dreamer stage of a process is on representing and widening the perception of a particular plan or idea. Its primary level of focus is on generating the content or the 'what' of the plan or idea. According to Disney, the function of a 'dreamer' is to "see clearly in his own mind how every piece of business in a story [or project] will be put." Dreamer objectives include: Stating the goal in positive terms and establishing the purpose and payoffs of the desired state.

To think like a Dreamer it is helpful to keep your head and eyes up, and get into a comfortable posture that is symmetrical and relaxed.

Realist

The purpose of the 'Realist' is to turn the dream into a workable plan or product. As a Realist, you want to act "as if" the dream is possible, and focus on the steps or actions required to actually reach the dream. Your primary focus should be on 'how' to implement the plan or idea.

The Realist phase of a process is more action oriented to moving towards the future, operating with respect to a shorter term time frame than the Dreamer. The Realist is often more focused on procedures or operations. His or her primary level of focus is on 'how' to implement the plan or idea.

To think like a 'Realist' it helps to sit with your head and eyes straight ahead or slightly forward with a posture that is symmetrical and slightly forward. Your cognitive focus should be to act 'as if' the dream is achievable and consider how the idea or plan can be implemented; emphasizing specific actions and defining short term steps. It also helps to put oneself into the "shoes" of the other people involved in the plan and perceive it from several points of view.

Critic

The Critic phase of creativity follows the Dreamer and Realist. The purpose of being a Critic is to evaluate the plan or project that has been proposed, and look for potential problems and 'missing links'. To be an effective Critic, it is important to take the perspectives of people who might influence, or be influenced by, the plan or project (either positively or negatively), and consider their needs and reactions. The primary purpose of the critic is to find potential problems and missing links in a particular plan or potential solution. The strategy of the critic is to help avoid problems by taking different perspectives and finding missing links by logically considering 'what would happen if' problems occur.

Thinking like a Critic involves taking on an angular posture, in which the eyes and head are down and slightly tilted, and touching your chin or face with one of your hands.

"Critics" are often considered the most difficult people to handle in an interaction because of their seemingly negative focus and their tendency to mismatch the ideas and suggestions of others. The most challenging problems occur when the Critic doesn't just criticize the dream or the plan, but begins to criticize the Dreamer and Realist. It is different to say, "That idea is stupid," than to say, "*You* are stupid for having that idea."

It is important to keep in mind that criticism, like all other behavior, is positively intended. The two most effective principles for dealing with a critic are 1) to find the positive purpose behind the criticism, and 2) to turn criticisms into questions. The following sequence is a good strategy to turn a criticism into a question:

1. What is your criticism or objection to the solution or the plan?
2. What is the positive intention behind the criticism?
3, Given that that's the intention, what is the question that you have about the dream or plan? Turn the criticism into a question. In particular, *what is the HOW question that goes with that question?*

Thinking Style	**Dreamer**	**Realist**	**Critic**
Level of Focus	What	How	Why
Representational Preference	Vision	Action	Logic
Approach	Toward	Toward	Away
Time Frame	Long Term	Short Term	Long/Short Term
Time Orientation	Future	Present	Past/Future
Reference	Internal - Self	External - Environment	External - Others
Mode of Comparison	Match	Match	Mismatch

Summary of the Key Cognitive Patterns Associated with Dreamer, Realist and Critic

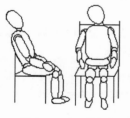

Dreamer State Physiology	**Realist State Physiology**	**Critic State Physiology**

Summary of the Key Physical Patterns Associated with Dreamer, Realist and Critic

Dreamer, Realist and Critic can also be associated with particular types of questions. The process described on the following page is a way to direct the process of a group through the stages of Dreamer, Realist and Critic by answering and exploring a range of questions appropriate for each phase. (See the books *Strategies of Genius, Volume I, Skills for the Future* and *Visionary Leadership Skills* for more ways to apply Dreamer, Realist and Critic in management.)

'Imagineering' Group Process

1. Write down your answers to the following questions about your project.

Dreamer:
   What is the purpose of the project?
   Who is the leader/group in relationship to the project?

Realist:
   What is the time frame of the project?
   Who are the actors?

Critic:
   Who might be positively or negatively affected by the project?
   Under what circumstances would the leader not do the project?

2. As the leader of your group, review aloud your project and the answers you gave to the questions above.

3. Lead the group in exploring the answers to the following questions, guiding them to the appropriate state for each set:

Dreamer:
   What are the potential benefits?
   What other possibilities are there?
   What else could the project lead to in the future?

Realist:
   What is the first/next step?
   What is evidence or feedback that you are making progress?
   What resources are available to assist in the project?

Critic:
   Why might someone object to the project?
   What are their needs or expectations?
   What is missing?

Chapter 7

Delegation

Overview of Chapter 7

- Modeling Leadership Skills For Delegation
- Information Gathering Methodology
- Patterns and Results
  - Key Considerations in Delegation
  - Logical Levels
  - Alignment
  - The Communication Matrix
- Applications and Tools
  - Communication/Delegation Exercise
  - Communication Strategies
  - Communication Strategy Exercise

Modeling Leadership Skills for Delegation

Delegation refers to assigning or communicating a task or activity to another person. Delegation can be classified as primarily an interactive skill, which is supported by certain communication and linguistic skills. The goal of this part of the leadership research study was to define the way that leaders: (1) prepared to delegate a particular task, and (2) managed the process of both verbal and non-verbal communication during the delegation interaction.

In contrast with the modeling of leadership skills in problem solving, which emphasized the way leaders managed a group, the study of delegation focused primarily on one-to-one interactions.

Information Gathering Methodology

The modeling process and sequence of modeling activities for the study of delegation was essentially the same as that followed for problem solving. The sequence of modeling activities included:

Initial Questionnaire

For the first activity, the participating managers filled out questionnaires relating to how they handled the process of delegation. Again, the questionnaire was designed to elicit information in the form of a T.O.T.E. - i.e., the goals, evidence procedures and operations used by the managers to assign or communicate tasks to their collaborators. The purpose of the questionnaires was to elicit and encourage general thinking about the situation so that common patterns with respect to delegation could be defined and shared by all of the participants.

The questionnaire was worded as follows:

1. Write a brief description of a typical example of a delegation situation in the context of your role in the company.

2. When you are in this kind of context and situation, what are the goals or objectives that guide your actions? (List them in short sentences or key words.)

3. What do you typically use as evidence to know you are accomplishing those goals?

4. What do you typically do to get to the goal - what are some specific steps and activities that you use to achieve your delegation goals in that context?

5. When you experience unexpected problems or difficulties in achieving your goals in this context, what specific activities or steps do you take?

6. Which, if any, of these delegation goals, evidence procedures or activities would change if the context of the delegation situation changed to an interaction with a small group or team instead of a single collaborator? How, specifically, would they change?

Written Scenario

Following the discussion of the questionnaire, a brief scenario defining a challenging delegation situation was distributed to the group members for discussion in small groups. The specific scenario given for discussion was:

You are the Director of Personnel for Company "B".
The company has introduced a new product for which
personnel is responsible for recruiting new support
staff. There is a meeting in two days of a project team
composed of your peers from marketing, finance,
information systems and customer relations. The
objective of the meeting is to discuss the requirements
for implementing a plan to release the new product.
Because of a family emergency you cannot make the
meeting and need to delegate the task of participating
in the meeting to your assistant.

How would you handle this situation?

Again, the results of the discussions were elicited and
tabulated with the full group. During the full group discussion of the results, potentially relevant distinctions were
introduced to the group and evaluated as to their significance.

Delegation Role Plays and Simulations

Following the scenarios, participants enacted role plays
and simulations that were relevant to their own personal
leadership contexts. The role plays and simulations were
conducted in a 'fish bowl' style, first with the whole group as
observers and then breaking into smaller experimental groups.
The role plays were run in such a way that there was the
option to substitute group members into the leadership role
so that differences and similarities between styles, skills and
use of tools could be identified and compared.

The following is an example of a role play/simulation that
was used to explore some of the interactive and relational
leadership skills (as well as the cognitive and linguistic
skills) associated with effective delegation:

Context

A commitment has been contracted with a client company by a training group/company to prepare a package destined for a large population of young employees. It consists of a series of instructional units which cover a wide range of topics which relate to: the macroenvironment of the company (macroeconomics), the microenvironment (competition, markets), the company's organizational system (and its functional units), the individuals (their roles and motivational subsystems).

The client has to be insured that the contents of each instructional unit is congruent with the others and that it is also congruent with company's strategies and policies.

The package must be multi-media (videos, texts, teaching manual), governed by a personal computer.

"A" is the head of the project. "A" has been given previous assignments which have already saturated his time, he has to entrust another consultant-trainer to coordinate 5 functional experts responsible for: (1) content, (2) videotapes (3) graphics (4) EDP software (5) testing procedures.

The budget is limited because part of it has already been spent in previous phases.

"B" has to undertake the responsibility of coordinating the functional experts in the execution of their tasks.

"A" is to delegate the project to "B" but will maintain a supervisory role, in addition to remaining as the primary interface with the client.

Observations of specific verbal and non-verbal communication patterns made by the person in the leadership role were made explicitly by the members of the research team during the role plays, as well as any patterns relating to specific NLP communication skills, such as psychogeography, tonal marking, non-verbal meta messages, the use of different representational channels, etc.

Similar measures as those applied during the problem solving study, in order to insure "code congruency," were applied during the delegation activities. That is, the participating managers were also asked to make comments on their observations, from the perspective of either being in the role play or as an observer. As the NLP distinctions were introduced, the research team members noted which ones seemed to be picked up and incorporated naturally in to the comments of the managers, and which ones seemed to be left aside.

The participants were also asked direct questions such as:

a. Are these effective/relevant distinctions to describe, release, learn, or transfer the skills of leadership?

b. Is this an effective instrument to get at what is the essence of leadership?

c. Does it "fit" - i.e., draw out or illuminate a structure that expands or enriches your leadership capabilities?

Patterns and Results

With respect to leadership within organizations, an initial general distinction may be made between delegation with respect to a) general institutional tasks and b) special or specific single operations.

General institutional tasks are defined to be those with a high amount of redundancy from the larger system - i.e., they are ongoing tasks and contexts that are accepted and understood by the whole system. One of the primary goals for the leaders with regard to delegating institutional tasks is the professional growth of the collaborator within the constraints of the task and its context. Other goals centering around the delegation of institutional tasks are: (1) defining technical tasks, (2) defining responsibility and (3) defining relationships. Generally, the evidence procedures employed for testing the success of institutional delegation focus around timing criteria related to the task and existing institutional controls.

Single operations may be defined as either new or one-time tasks, and may be subdivided further into either: (1) technical or (2) organizational operations. Technical operations may be further divided into those which were quantitative and can be assessed quantitatively, and those which are more qualitative. The evidence procedures for single operation delegation need to be done on a more 'ad hoc' basis than institutional tasks. While defining technical tasks, responsibility and relationships are important for the single operation delegation, and the alignment and fit of that task into the larger framework of the system is priorital.

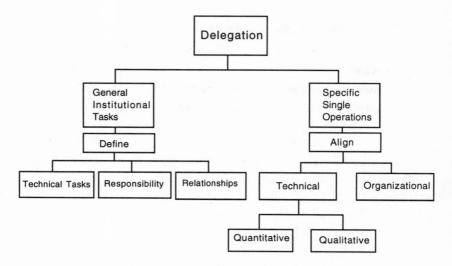

**Some Key Distinctions and Issues Related to
Delegation**

Key Considerations in Delegation

The two most important processes involved in delegation can be characterized as (a) *defining* the 'problem space' involved in the task to be delegated, and (b) *aligning* the various individuals and levels of processes required by the task. Some key considerations relating to these processes of delegation include:

1. Determining "need to know" versus "need not to know" - i.e., how much of the 'problem space' of a situation does the collaborator to whom one is delegating a task need to know about?

a. The "problem space" relevant to delegation may include factors such as: the 'status' of individuals involved in the task, the amount of risk (if any), possible competition, etc.

b. A belief of many of the managers involved in the study was that "there should be no secret information in a company." As one leader pointed out, "If my collaborator becomes aware of something through a different channel than me, then I lose leadership." (The leader appears to know less than the person to whom he is delegating.) Another leader added, "I've got to work as if people know, even though they don't know."

2. Determining who else in the company needs to be informed of the delegation. It can be confusing, and even demoralizing, if other team members, collaborators, or people in related roles in an organization, are surprised to discover that someone has been delegated a particular activity, and they did not know about it. The person who has received the delegation, in essence becomes a "delegate," with the accompanying responsibilities and authority. Thus it is important to inform other parts of the system that may be affected or influenced by the delegation of a particular task.

3. Ensuring the alignment of the key individuals and levels of processes involved in the activity necessary to accomplish the task. One of the main functions of delegation is to ensure alignment along two parameters: (1) to align the perceptual space of collaborators or team members to the problem space encompassed by the task to be accomplished, and (2) to align the various levels of activity related to the task to be supportive of one another - so that the 'when' and 'where' of the task (environment) is congruent with the 'what' (behavior), and that the 'how' is congruent/aligned with the 'why' and 'who' that defined the purpose of the task. This raises the importance of "logical levels" with respect to delegation.

Logical Levels

The concept of logical levels of learning and change was initially formulated as a mechanism in the behavioral sciences by Gregory Bateson (1972), based on the work of Russell and Whitehead in mathematics. The concept of "neuro-logical levels" was formulated by the author as a way to operationally apply Bateson's concept of logical levels and logical types to human communication and change.

Logical levels essentially refers to a fundamental hierarchy of organization, in which each level is progressively more encompassing and impactful psychologically. Any system of activity, for instance, is a subsystem embedded inside of another system which is embedded inside of another system, and so on. This kind of relationship between systems produces different levels of processes, relative to the system in which one is operating.

In our brain structure, language, and perceptual systems, there are natural hierarchies or levels of experience. The effect of each level is to organize and control the information on the level below it. Changing something on an upper level would necessarily change things on the lower levels; changing something on a lower level could but would not necessarily effect the upper levels. Gregory Bateson identified four basic levels of learning and change—each level more abstract than the level below it but each having a greater degree of impact on the individual. These levels roughly correspond to:

The Larger System	Vision & Purpose	Who Else?
Sense of Identity and Role	Mission	Who?
Belief and Value Systems	Permission & Motivation	Why?
Capabilities	Maps & Plans	How?
Specific Behaviors	Actions & Reactions	What?
Environment	External Context	Where? When?

The environment level involves the specific external conditions in which our behavior takes place. Behaviors without any inner map, plan or strategy to guide them, however, are like knee jerk reactions, habits or rituals. At the level of capability we are able to select, alter and adapt a class of behaviors to a wider set of external situations. At the level of beliefs and values, we may encourage, inhibit or generalize a particular strategy, plan or way of thinking. Identity, of course, consolidates whole systems of beliefs and values into a sense of self. While each level becomes more abstracted from the specifics of behavior and sensory experience, it actually has a more and more widespread effect on our behavior and experience. In summary:

* *Environmental factors* determine the external opportunities or constraints a person has to react to. Answer to the questions **where?** and **when?**

* *Behavior* is made up of the specific actions or reactions taken within the environment. Answer to the question **what?**

* *Capabilities* guide and give direction to behavioral actions through a mental map, plan or strategy. Answer to the question **how?**

* *Beliefs* and *values* provide the reinforcement (motivation and permission) that supports or denies capabilities. Answer to the question **why?**

* *Identity* factors determine overall purpose (mission) and shape beliefs and values through our sense of self. Answer to the question **who?**

* *System* issues relate to the fact that we are a part of a larger system that reaches beyond ourselves as individuals to teams, groups, professional community and even global systems. Answer to the question **who else?**

Alignment

Alignment is a key property of effective planning, problem solving and leadership. In an effective system, the actions and outcomes of individuals within their micro environments are congruent with their strategies and goals. These goals, in turn, are congruent with the system's culture and mission with respect to the macro environment. In other words, there is an internal alignment of the individual with his or her vision, and another level of alignment with the community in which a person will attempt to achieve his or her vision.

Thus, there are three types of alignment: 1) personal alignment, in which there is a congruity between all parts of an individual, 2) alignment of supporting processes with respect to a goal or vision, 3) environmental alignment, in which the goals and actions of individuals or groups fit congruently and ecologically with the larger system (environment, organization, community, culture, etc.).

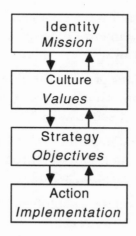

Levels of Processes in a System

Systems are made up of both 'hierarchical' levels and 'logical' levels of interaction. Thus, in a functional system:

1) The relationship between the members of the system supports the task to be accomplished.
2) There is a shared perception of the levels, perceptual positions and time frames relevant to the problem space and solution space associated with the task.
3) There is an alignment of the various logical levels related to the task.
4) There is a congruence and alignment of the outcomes of the relevant actors involved in the system. (In a hierarchical or complementary system this is expressed through the ease by which tasks are delegated to the appropriate roles. In a peer or symmetrical system, this is expressed through the ease by which people are able to negotiate and reach consensus about tasks and outcomes.)
5) The actions of individuals are aligned with the mission associated with their role.

In other words, there are a number of different types of alignment related to task and relationship. Types of alignment related to tasks involve:

• The professional and perceptual space of the relevant actors with the problem space to be addressed.
• The perceptual spaces of the relevant actors with one another.
• The levels involved in the task or goal.
• The levels of communication between the relevant actors.

Types of alignment related to relationship involve:

• The different levels of a person within their role.
• Levels of experience between people in different roles.
• Levels between different parts of a person.

To be effective in a particular system, an individual must understand the relationship between the various levels of change, and align his or her activities to fit those dynamics. That is, goals and actions on an individual level should support the functional objectives and strategy related to role, which in turn should be congruent with culture and identity, and mission with respect to the larger environment.

Alignment also relates to where stability and variation are placed in a system. When one part of a system needs to be kept stable, other parts must necessarily vary and adapt in order to help maintain stability. Consistency at one level requires flexibility at other levels.

Perceptual Space ——— Align ——→ Problem Space

```
          a.  Identity      Who?              ⎤
 ↑        b.  Beliefs/Values Why?             ⎥  Qualitative
 ┊        c.  Capabilities   How?             ⎦
Align     d.  Behavior       What?            ⎤
 ┊        e.  Environment    Where/When?      ⎦  Quantitative
```

Alignment is a Key Outcome of Effective Delegation

The need for alignment is a naturally occurring experience. When the various levels of information required for an activity have not been defined ahead of time, people often intuitively and spontaneously request them. Consider the hypothetical conversation below, between a manger and his or her collaborator.

Manager: Do you have Tuesday afternoon free to meet with me in my office? (Proposes 'when' and 'where'.)

Collaborator: Yes. What do you want to meet about?

Manager: I'd like to get together with you to prepare for our presentation next week. (Defines 'what' is to be done.)

Collaborator: How specifically do you want to 'prepare'?

Manager: I thought we might go over the sequence of information we're planning to present and see if we will need to make any visual aids. (Defines 'how' the process will take place.)

Collaborator: Why? Do you think it is going to be difficult for people to understand our point?

Manager: Well, I believe it is good to have key ideas represented in several different ways. (Defines the reasons behind the 'how' and the 'what'.)

Collaborator: Alright. Do you want me to be mainly in the role of a co-developer, or should I be ready to play 'devil's advocate'?

Manager: It might be a good idea for you to put yourself into the shoes of our audience, and perceive the presentation as if you were one of them. (Defines 'whose' perspectives are to be taken.)

While this conversation is hypothetical, interactions just like it probably occur many times a day in companies. A complete delegation would involve specifying the where, when, what, how, why, who and who else, related to the task or activity being delegated. If a particular aspect is left out, that information will be either requested or assumed by the collaborator (and if his or her assumptions are erroneous, it can cause trouble).

In fact, many of the leaders participating in the study maintained that one important measure of the maturity of a collaborator related to which levels of process the leader had to explicitly define for the collaborator, and which levels they could leave for the collaborator to complete on his or her own.

A leader may choose to define the where, when, what, and why of a particular activity for instance, and let the collaborator determine how. For a more mature collaborator, the leader may define what is to be done and the role the collaborator is to have in that activity (the who), and allow the collaborator to decide the where, when, how and why.

One of the most essential cognitive skills of delegation involves the ability to define the levels of process involved in the particular task or activity to be delegated, and then to determine how much of that information to explicitly provide for the collaborator being assigned the task. If a mature collaborator is given too much explicit direction, for example, he or she can feel constrained, under utilized or even demotivated.

The Communication Matrix

The most important interactive skills of delegation are those relating to verbal and non-verbal communication. The *Communication Matrix* (Dilts, 1996) is a simple but useful model of communication which can help people to both understand the process of communication better and to develop more effective communication skills. According to Shannon and Weaver (1948), effective communication includes a source (the speaker); an encoder (the vocal system); a message (language and visual cues); a channel (sound waves in the air); a decoder (the listener's ears); and a receiver (the listener). Effective communication must also address issues of noise (static on a radio; background noise in face-to-face communication).

The communication matrix incorporates these basic elements of communication theory into a practical model of face-to-face communication. According to the communication matrix, communication involves people sending messages to one another through various media. Thus, the three basic elements involved in any process of human communication are: (1) people, (2) messages and (3) the medium through which the messages are being sent.

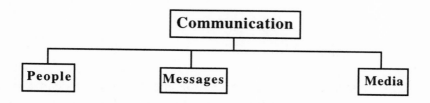

Basic Elements Involved in Communication

The simplest case of communication, for instance, would involve two people sending and receiving messages from one another through the medium of the spoken word. The two would alternate at various times between (a) the 'sender' or 'transmitter' of various types of messages and (b) the 're-ceiver' of various types of messages from the other. As the two people interact, in addition to spoken language, they may at times also draw diagrams, make gestures or refer to written material as a medium for the various messages they are attempting to transmit.

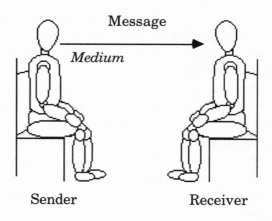

A 'Sender' Transmits a Message to a 'Receiver'

People - Internal Dimensions

The internal aspect of people that most influences commu-nication is their state. The internal states of both sender and receiver impact the flow of the communication. States act as both a filter and a bias in receiving and interpreting mes-sages. A person's internal state is typically a function of his or her attitude and thinking style.

Attitudes, such as "confidence," "concern," "openness," "enthusiasm," "curiosity," etc., are often more temporary and may shift during an interaction. In fact, sometimes the purpose of a communication is to attempt to shift the attitude of others. Attitudes are influenced by both mental and physical processes and are often reflected in certain physical cues, such as body posture, gestures and head orientation.

Thinking styles, such as 'Dreamer', 'Realist' and 'Critic', are more associated with an individual's personality and tend to be more constant during an interaction. Rather than be changed, different thinking styles need to be acknowledged and addressed in some way. Different thinking styles are characterized by what are known as 'meta program patterns' in NLP.

Attitudes and thinking styles determine the 'chemistry' of the interaction; i.e., whether it will be volatile, stable, sluggish, etc. In addition to recognizing and managing his or her own internal state in an interaction, it is often essential for leaders to take into account the states of others. Communicating to a group of 'concerned critics' can be quite different from communicating with a group of 'enthusiastic dreamers'. And, depending upon one's outcomes, both present their own unique challenges.

People - Relational Dimensions

The relational dimension of people involved in a communication has to do with their roles or 'status' with respect to one another. In organizations and social systems, issues of 'status' can be quite influential and also fairly complex at times. There are several fundamental types of status: complementary, symmetrical and reciprocal. A 'complementary' relationship is one in which the role of one person "complements" that of the other - such as subordinate to boss, a student to a teacher or a child to a parent. Complementary relationships are often a function of organizational or social hierarchies. 'Symmetrical' relationships are essentially peer relationships, in which people are in similar roles and treat each other as 'equals'. 'Reciprocal' relationships are those in which the people involved periodically "pass the baton" or trade roles during the interaction. In a team interaction, for instance, individuals may trade off "leading" the team at various times. Thus, in a reciprocal relationship, individuals may at various times be "boss", "subordinate", "teacher", "student", etc.

There is one other basic type of "status" that is relevant in leadership situations, which could be called "meta-complementary". A meta-complementary relationship is like that of a consultant to a client. On the one hand, the consultant is "working for" the client (in this sense the client is the "boss"). On the other hand, however, the consultant's job is to direct the behavior of the client (in this sense the consultant is the "boss" in certain ways).

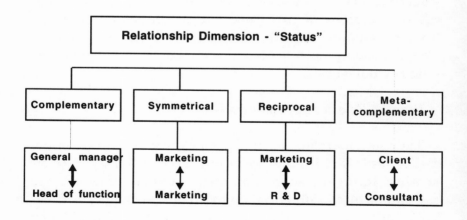

Different types of messages and media are often used to acknowledge and adapt to different types of status. Many languages, for example, have both a formal and familiar version of the word "you" to acknowledge the difference between complementary and symmetrical relationships. Other verbal acknowledgments of relationships involve the use of words like "sir" or "madam" and the use of a person's last name or first name to establish 'status'. Similarly, different media are often used to acknowledge different types of status. A phone call indicates a different type of status than a formally written document or a letter sent by courier.

'State' and 'status' are also important to consider together during a communication interaction. For instance, it is quite a different situation for an enthusiastic subordinate to communicate to a skeptical boss than for an enthusiastic boss to communicate to a skeptical subordinate.

Intended Versus Received Messages

In considering the 'message' element of communication, a first distinction needs to be made between the 'intended' message and the 'received' message. In NLP there is a saying that "the meaning of your communication is the response you elicit; regardless of what you intended to communicate." In other words, the 'meaning' of a message to the receiver is what that individual 'receives', irrespective of the intent of the sender. This statement is an acknowledgment that the message intended by the sender is not always the message that is received by the others involved in the interaction. One of the most important communication skills is insuring that the message you intended is the one that was received. As a business leader once said, "The challenge is to get people to do what you wanted, not what you said." In essence, effective communication is a feedback loop between sender(s) and receiver(s) which attempts to optimize the congruence between the intended and received messages.

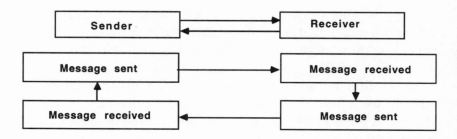

Feedback Loop Between 'Sender' and 'Receiver'

Messages and Meta Messages

The content of a message is generally accompanied by higher level 'meta messages' (often non-verbal) that give emphasis or provide cues for how to interpret the message. In many cases, the 'content' relates to the purely verbal aspect of the communication, while meta messages relate to the non-verbal portion of the communication. Meta messages are messages about other messages. While two messages may contradict one another, meta messages are on a different 'level' than the content. As an example, a leader may tell a group to "Pay attention" while pointing to his or her eyes. This gesture would be considered a "meta message" indicating how the group is to pay attention (i.e., by watching). If the leader were pointing to his or her ears, it would indicate a different mode of paying attention.

Using a yellow highliter to mark out key phrases in a text is another example of a meta message. Punctuation also serves as a meta message. Changing a question mark to an exclamation point, shifts the meaning of the rest of the message. Even the medium through which a message is sent can be a meta message. A message sent by fax or courier would indicate an urgency with respect to task. A phone call or personal meeting would place an emphasis more on the relational aspects of the message contents.

The function of a meta message is basically to inform the listener as to what 'type' of message is about to be delivered or has been delivered, and how to best 'receive' that message. In other words, meta messages are necessary in order to 'decode' the 'meaning' of a message. Thus, the same message will have different meanings if accompanied by different meta messages.

As an analogy, when one computer is communicating with another it needs to send certain 'control characters' along with the actual text it is transmitting. The control characters are meta messages informing the other computer what kind of data it is sending and where to place it in its memory.

Levels of Messages

The purpose of meta messages is often to clarify at which 'level' the content of a message has been sent or received. As an example, if a leader gives a collaborator the verbal message, "You made a mistake," it could be interpreted in several different ways. Is this message intended to be focused at the level of identity or behavior? In other words, is the leader indicating disappointment in the person or simply giving feedback about a particular action? This type of information is often critical for the proper interpretation of a communication. Clearly the message "you made a mistake" takes on a completely different meaning if the meta message is "I want to help you do better" than if the meta message is "I am angry at you."

Such information is often communicated through non-verbal cues such as voice inflection. The statement, "*You* made a mistake," is more likely to be interpreted as an indication that the collaborator has done something wrong and is in trouble. The statement, "You *made a mistake*," on the other hand, would be more likely to indicate an emphasis on an event or the correctness of a procedure rather than the person.

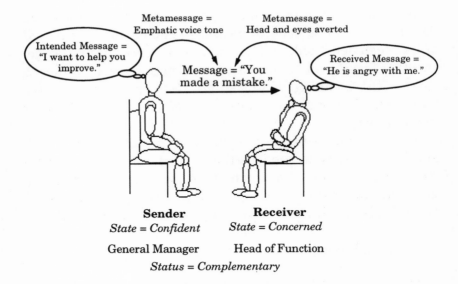

Metamessage =
Emphatic voice tone

Metamessage =
Head and eyes averted

Intended Message =
"I want to help you
improve."

Message = "You
made a mistake."

Received Message =
"He is angry with me."

Sender
State = Confident

General Manager

Receiver
State = Concerned

Head of Function

Status = Complementary

Elements Influencing the Type of Message Received

Because meta messages are typically communicated non-verbally, they are often outside of the awareness of both the sender and the receiver. Developing the awareness to read and monitor meta messages is probably one of the most essential communication skills.

Sometimes, however, it is necessary to be very explicit about the particular levels of processes being addressed in a communication. In this case, it important to know that there are also different verbal cues associated with different levels of experience:

- Identity is associated with language like: "I am a ..." or "He is a ..." or "You are a ..."

- Belief level language is often in the form of statements of judgments, rules and cause effect, e.g. "if ... then ..." "one should ..." "we have to ..."

- The level of capabilities is indicated by words such as "know", "how", "I am able", "think", etc.

- Behavioral levels language refers to specific behaviors and observable actions, e.g. 'do', 'act', walk, say, etc.

- Language at the environmental level refers to specific observable features or details in one's external context e.g. "white paper," "10:30 in the morning," "large room," etc.

Media - Channels of Communication

Clearly, all messages must be transmitted through some kind of medium. The various media through which a message can be conveyed have different constraints and strengths which influence how the message is sent and received. In organizations, the medium through which a message is sent is made up of:

1) the channel of communication,
2) the context of the communication,
3) the cultural framework surrounding the communication.

Channels of communication are related to the different sensory modalities by which a message may be represented. The context and cultural framework surrounding the communication relate to the types of assumptions and inferences which will be used to give meaning to the communication. Effective communication involves determining the sequence and mix of channels to be used to transmit messages. It also involves considering the meaning of the various channels within the context and the cultural framework in which messages are being sent.

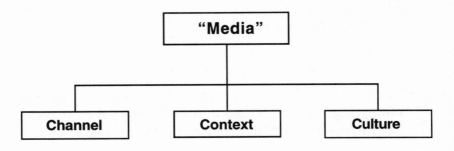

The representational channels selected for communication are particularly important for delegation from the NLP perspective. Our abilities to communicate and understand messages come from our capability to make maps in our minds. We build our mental maps out of information from the five senses or 'representational systems': sight, sound, feeling, taste, and smell. Our senses constitute the form or structure of thinking as opposed to its content. Every thought that you have, regardless of its content, is going to be a function of pictures, sounds, feelings, smells or tastes, and how those representations relate to one another. We are constantly linking together sensory representations to build and update our maps of reality. We create these maps based on feedback from our sensory experience.

"Representational channels" relate to the senses and the type of sensory modality or representation a person is using to either send or receive a message. When someone is speaking out loud, he or she is using a verbal channel of external representation. A more visual or symbolic form of external representation would involve drawing or displaying symbols and diagrams. When a person interactively demonstrates an activity or "walks someone else through it," he or she is using a more physical channel of communication.

Similarly, when a person is receiving a communication he or she may be more focused on sights, sounds or feelings.

Thus, the selection of the channel of communication may be made based on the thinking style and focus of attention of the receiver.

The basic types of representational channels involved in communication include:

• Verbal   • Written   • Pictorial   • Physical

Different modalities of representation have different strengths. The verbal mode of representation, for instance, has a lot of strengths in terms of how information is sequenced with respect to logical dependencies. The visual channel is often the best way to synthesize information into a whole or 'gestalt'. Acting out an idea or concept physically brings out its concrete aspects.

Emphasizing different channels of communication and representation can lead people into different types of thinking styles. For example, the visual channel helps to stimulate imaginative thinking. The verbal channel is often most effective for logical or critical thinking. Focusing on physical channels influences people toward an action orientation.

Different representational channels can also influence people's relationship to information. For instance, writing something down on a flip chart is a simple way of encouraging consensus, because once an idea is expressed on paper the person who proposed the idea is not so intimately associated with the idea anymore. Externalizing an idea allows you to separate the *what* from the *who*.

Different modalities of representation have different strengths. The verbal mode of internal representation, for instance, has a lot of strengths in terms of how information is sequenced with respect to logical dependencies. The visual channel is often the best way to synthesize information into a whole or 'gestalt'. Acting out an idea or concept physically brings out its concrete aspects.

Applications and Tools

The following exercise provides a way to practice some of the key cognitive, interactive and linguistic skills of leadership in the context of delegation. The exercise involves applying various aspects of the Communication Matrix by explicitly constructing a particular message involving various levels of information, communicating it to another person, and then contrasting the various levels of "message" the person received with the messages that were intended.

Communication/Delegation Exercise

The Communicator is to identify a task or activity that is important for him or her to be able to communicate/ delegate effectively to others.

Phase I

The Communicator is to plan a presentation by defining his or her 'intended message' incorporating the following levels of information:

a. *Where - the context or environment in which the task or activity is to be carried out.*

b. *When - the time frame in which the task or activity is to be completed.*

c. *What - the behavioral actions or objectives required by the task or activity .*

d. *How - conceptual or strategic guidelines for conducting the task or activity .*

e. *Why - the criteria, values or beliefs which are the motives for the task and are to be upheld by the task or activity.*

f. *Who - information regarding key roles, role identity or status issues related to the task or activity .*

The Communicator is also to consider which non-verbal signals will be evidence that the messages are being received at the intended levels.

Phase II

The Communicator has 5-10 minutes to present the task or activity to role player(s) representing the intended receiver(s). When the Communicator has finished the presentation, the receiver(s) records the 'received' message by filling out the information sheet below.

a. *What is the context or environment in which the task or activity is to be carried out? (Where)*

b. *What is the time frame in which the task or activity is to be completed? (When)*

c. *What are the behavioral actions or objectives required by the task or activity? (What)*

d. *What are the conceptual or strategic guidelines for conducting the task or activity? (How)*

e. *What criteria, values or beliefs are the motives for the task and are to be upheld by the task or activity? (Why)*

f. What are the key roles, role identity or status issues related to the task or activity? (Who)

Phase III

The Communicator and receiver compare the intended and received messages and discuss the reasons for any discrepancies. The group should consider the influence of both verbal and non-verbal communication patterns, and discuss which other representational channels could be used to communicate the task or activity. They can also reflect on how the states of the Communicator and receivers influenced the interpretation of various messages and cues.

Communication Strategies

When delegation involves more than one person, such as when a team leader is delegating a task to an entire team, the interactive skills of the leader revolve around his or her communication strategy. 'Communication strategies' relate to managing the entire mix of elements defined by the communication matrix while communicating a task or objective to an individual or group.

There are several classes of activities related to one's communication strategy:

1) Determining the general message and 'chunking' it into the content elements and meta messages.

2) Establishing the current and desired state, status and context in which the messages and meta messages are to be sent.

3) Determining by what channels message and meta message elements will be most effectively transmitted.

4) Recognizing and responding to feedback about how messages and meta messages are being received by others.

A communication strategy involves elements which are preplanned and aspects which are selected or adopted in response to feedback. The preplanned aspects of a communication strategy essentially relate to how information is prepared and delivered. For example, having the same message in a written report and on a transparency is a meta message about the significance of the information. Whether printed material is given at the beginning of a meeting or handed out during the progression of the meeting is a meta message about how to perceive that information with respect to the other information that has been presented.

The dynamic aspect of managing messages involves the continuous monitoring of how messages are being sent and received - i.e., the ability to adapt one's messages and meta messages according to the responses received as reactions to other messages. Messages may be 'adapted' via:

1) Using observational skill and feedback to reduce distortions between intended and received messages.

2) Determining the selection and combination of messages and meta messages.

3) Ensuring that the micro messages support the larger message and lead in the direction of the communication outcome.

Communication Strategy Exercise

The following exercise provides a way to practice and explore some of the various aspects of forming a Communication Strategy. It involves contrasting both intended and received verbal messages and non-verbal meta messages. The exercise involves the following steps:

1. Get into a group of four and choose roles for a role play made up of: 1) Team Leader, 2) Dreamer, 3) Realist and 4) Critic.
   e.g. Marketing: Team Leader
   Research: Dreamer
   Production: Realist
   Finance: Critic

2. The general objective for the team leader (who is to be the primary "communicator" during the role play) is to effectively and clearly describe a project to the other team members. Before beginning the role play, the team leader should choose a 'project' (e.g., a new bicycle, a training program, a computer game, etc.) and take a few minutes to fill in the *Intended Message Worksheet*.

3. The leader then has 5-10 minutes to describe the project to the receivers.

4. When the team leader has finished defining the project, each of the team members is to individually record what message and meta messages they received by filling in the *Received Message Worksheet*. The team leader and the other role players then contrast the leader's 'intended' message and meta messages with the messages and meta messages 'received' by the group members.

Intended Message Worksheet

a. *Where – the context or environment in which the task or activity is to be carried out.*

b. *When – the time frame in which the task or activity is to be completed.*

c. *What – the behavioral actions or objectives required by the task or activity .*

d. *How – conceptual or strategic guidelines for conducting the task or activity .*

e. *Why – the criteria, values or beliefs which are the motives for the task and are to be upheld by the task or activity.*

f. *Who – information regarding key roles, role identity or status issues related to the task or activity .*

Intended Meta Messages

State – *What state do/did you want to be in as a leader?*

Key non-verbal cues:

Status – *What kind of relationship do/did you want to have with the team?*

Key non-verbal cues:

Level of focus - *Which logical level(s) do/did you most want to emphasize?*

Key non-verbal cues:

Context - *What values and/or criteria are most significant for accomplishing the project?*

Key non-verbal cues:

Received Message Worksheet

a. What is the context or environment in which the task or activity is to be carried out? (Where)

b. What is the time frame in which the task or activity is to be completed? (When)

c. What are the behavioral actions or objectives required by the task or activity? (What)

d. What are the conceptual or strategic guidelines for conducting the task or activity? (How)

e. What criteria, values or beliefs are the motives for the task and are to be upheld by the task or activity? (Why)

f. What are the key roles, role identity or status issues related to the task or activity? (Who)

Received Meta Message

State - *What is the state of the leader?*

Key non-verbal cues:

Status - *What kind of relationship does the leader want to have with the team?*

Key non-verbal cues:

Level of focus - *Which logical level was most emphasized by the leader?*

Key non-verbal cues:

Context - *What values and/or criteria are most significant for accomplishing the project?*

Key non-verbal cues:

5. When the team leader and group members have compared the intended and received messages, the whole group is to reflect on the team leader's presentation and discuss what aspects of the leader's communication strategy were most effective.

Chapter 8

Training on the Job

Overview of Chapter 8

- **Modeling Leadership Skills For Training on the Job**
- **Information Gathering Methodology**
- **Patterns and Results**
  - **Summary of Key Leadership Skills**
  - **Basic Perceptual Positions in Communication and Relationships**
  - **Psychogeography**
- **Applications and Tools**
  - **The Meta Map**
  - **Making a Meta Map for Leadership**
  - **Leadership Role Play/Simulation Exercise**

Modeling Leadership Skills for Training on the Job

Training on the job has been defined as a process of 'permanent education', implying that it is an activity that never ends. Training on the job is a complex activity involving a combination of leadership abilities, including interactive, cognitive and linguistic skills. To effectively train a collaborator, a leader must variously act as a teacher, coach, and role model. One of the challenges of training on the job is that it incorporates a number of other important leadership skills, including problem solving and delegation The goal of this part of the leadership research study was to define the way that leaders: (1) conceptualized and approached the task of training collaborators on the job, and (2) achieved particular outcomes considered essential to the process of 'on the job training'.

A particular area to be addressed in the modeling of leadership skills with respect to 'training on the job', which was different from the study of problem solving and delegation, involved issues relating to the interface between (a) the leader and his or her collaborators with (b) other roles, groups and functions within the larger system of the organization.

Information Gathering Methodology

The modeling process and sequence of modeling activities for the study of training on the job was essentially the same as that followed for problem solving and delegation, with a few exceptions. In place of the written scenario, the participants were asked to fill in an additional questionnaire, specifying particular goals that had emerged in relation to training on the job. These goals were derived from the interviews made during the initial phase of the leadership research project. Additionally, more emphasis was placed on the interactive role plays. The participating managers were involved in designing the role plays and simulations used to explore the leadership skills associated with this capability.

Thus, the sequence of modeling activities included:

Initial Questionnaire

1. Write a brief description of a typical example of a job training situation in the context of your role in the company.

2. When you are in this kind of context and situation, what are the goals or objectives that guide your actions? (List them in short sentences or key words.)

3. What do you typically use as evidence to know you are accomplishing those goals?

4. What do you typically do to get to the goal - what are some specific steps and activities that you use to achieve your job training goals in that context?

5. When you experience unexpected problems or difficulties in achieving your goals in this context, what specific activities or steps do you take?

6. Which, if any, of these job training goals, evidence procedures or activities would change if the context of the job training situation changed to an interaction with a small group of subordinates instead of a single subordinate? How, specifically, would they change?

Second Questionnaire

Below are a list of goals and objectives for training a collaborator on the job. These goals were elicited from interviews with other effective leaders in the study. Please write a brief description of how, specifically, you accomplish each of these goals (provided it applies) in the context of your role in the company. Also, write a brief description of a) what evidence you use to know when to take action, and b) what evidence lets you know you have been successful with those actions.

1. *Goal:* Communicating your values and ethics as a leader.
   Operations:

   Evidence:

2. *Goal:* Work initiation - showing the collaborator what to do.
   Operations:

   Evidence:

3. *Goal:* Making job criteria explicit.
   Operations:

   Evidence:

4. *Goal:* Teaching context - i.e., setting boundaries and introducing them to the kind of world they will be working in.
   Operations:

   Evidence:

5. *Goal:* Monitoring job effectiveness.
   Operations:

   Evidence:

6. *Goal:* Giving reinforcements (positive and negative)
   Operations:

   Evidence:

Role Plays and Simulations for Training on the Job

Participants were asked to design and enact role plays and simulations that were relevant to the process of training on the job in their own personal leadership contexts. As with the previous topics of the study, the role plays and simulations were conducted in a 'fish bowl' style, first with the whole group as observers and then breaking into smaller experimental groups.

It is interesting to note that the role plays spontaneously constructed by the managers to explore leadership in this context had a unique structure. All of the role plays ended up being composed of three successive phases. In the first phase, the leader had to interact with his or her collaborator in order to delegate and "train" the person to handle a particular task or activity. During the second phase, the leader had to leave the room, and the collaborator was engaged in a situation relating to the task or activity presented by the leader in the first phase. The success of the collaborator in this situation was based on the effectiveness of the leader's skills in having prepared or trained the collaborator appropriately. In the third phase of the role play, the leader was brought back into the room, and had to deal with an unexpected challenge involving the participation of his or her collaborator. The ease or difficulty in addressing the challenge was determined by the results of his or own leadership ability in having trained his or her collaborator appropriately.

The following are some examples of the types of role play/ simulation created by the managers:

ROLE PLAY 1 - Implementing Leadership Skills

Roles:

1. General Director
2. Director of Marketing
3. Product Manager

Context:

The General Director has been given the task to implement a new style or skill set of leadership within his organization. The General Director is to train his or her collaborator, the Marketing director, in this style/skill set. The Marketing director is to in turn train his or her own collaborator, the Product Manager. The General Manager then is given the task to provide an implementation plan to open a new market for the Product Manager's product, which is not very profitable, within 10 days. This requires the allocation of certain resources that come in conflict with the Marketing manager's budget restrictions.

All three must meet to plan the implementation.

If all three are able to be congruent with the new leadership skill/style, the meeting should go more smoothly. The General Manager is under pressure to be congruent with the new style that he or she has initiated.

Phases:

I. General Director trains the Marketing Manager in a new leadership style/skill and delegates the task of implementing it with his or her Product Manager.

II. The Marketing Manager trains his Product Manager in the same skill/style.

III. The three meet together to solve the problem of the implementation plan.

(The problem of the Implementation plan is not given until the last phase of the role play.)

ROLE PLAY 2 - Presenting a Training Plan

Roles:
1. Personnel Director
2. Collaborator of Personnel Director
3. Chief of Production

Context:

Production has been experiencing difficulties with defective materials (approximately $100,000.00 per year) and high absenteeism. Top management has asked for an intervention from the Personnel Division to help address the problem.

The Chief of Production is under a time constraint because of intense demand and tends to highlite the technical aspects of the problem. Also, he is concerned that the plan not take up too much of his own budget, and wants to share the cost if possible.

The Director of Personnel wants to implement longer term training to maintain standards through time (which is also a strategic goal for top management).

The Collaborator is new to personnel and has only been working for a short time, and wants to make a good impression on his or her new boss.

(It is best if none of the role players know of the constraints and criteria of the others - with the exception of the initial quality problem.)

Phases:

I. The personnel director delegates to the collaborator the task of defining a training plan with the chief of production.

II. The collaborator interacts with the chief of production to define a plan.

III. All three characters meet under a time constraint to try to come up with a consensus about the intervention plan.

To get a sense of the character and dynamics of the role plays conducted during the modeling process, consider the following transcript of the role play described above:

DP = Director of Personnel
C = Collaborator
CP = Chief of Production

PHASE I (Director of Personnel and his collaborator)

The Director of Personnel has begun by setting the frames that it is more and more difficult to motivate people, and that the working context in the company are changing. In doing so he has emphasized the importance of consensus and the need for training. He has also acknowledged that this is the first real assignment to be given to the collaborator.

Director of Personnel: How have you been getting along so far?

Collaborator: I am finding my way.

DP: I know that you have the skills. Let me review the criteria and then give you some space for questions. Then your task is to submit a plan to me and the chief of production.

The purpose is to avoid problems this plan might give production since they are going through a time of intense demand. But we can't afford to wait.

The client is the company - in order to keep standards through time we need training. This is a strategic goal for top management.

C: Did top management produce any documentation about this problem?"

DP: There is a suspicion that it has to do with the lack of knowledge of repetitive tasks within the process. Let's give people awareness - if everyone behaves the same way, it will insure quality.

C: If the problem is one of motivation?

DP: What is the professional problem – relations among working groups and communication between them? Analyze the problem with the Chief of Production.

C: What if I tell him there is something not working in production?...Do I go to him as a partner or what?

DP: He is aware of the problems. Because he is Chief of Production he is not going to want to implement this training plan short term. I am interested in trying to convince him and get his consensus short term so that when we start the plan, he is not going to interfere.

C: My problem is starting from a shared basis. I would like to go through the documents already shared.

DP: He realizes there is a lot of defective material that does not pass the test and that there is a big problem of absenteeism.

C: Perfect! (Stands up, as if ready to go.)

(Following the interaction, the Director of Personnel commented to the group that he felt the Collaborator said "Perfect" too quickly – the Collaborator may have been comfortable with the situation but he was not.)

PHASE II (Collaborator and Chief of Production)

Chief of Production: Welcome. You are making my job easier. If you propose training you will find that I will happy about it. I don't have experience in that area. What do you suggest?

Collaborator: I have some information from my director but I would like to hear your point of view.

CP: So your boss didn't give you my point of view?

C: I know that there are some problems with rejected and incomplete material and a high rate of absenteeism. This could be caused by two things; 1) motivation and commitment or 2) professional preparation for specific tasks.

CP: This is a wide view. Why didn't you widen the field and involve the leaders?

C: Involving the leaders is my point of view as well.

CP: I'd like to add my impression to yours – improve team leaders. Do you have any experience in this field?

C: Certainly....not in this particular area because I am new.

CP: But your function has it?

C: Certainly, I would imagine.

CP: Under these conditions I think there is something we can do, because I think this is a classical problem.

C: Let me get you the documentation. But if you let me participate in the project I can do interviews and ask questions and submit a plan and analysis to you. Can you point out the important people to me?

CP: Wait a minute. I want to know how much this is going to cost and what the expected profit is compared to loss, etc. before I'm going to involve people. Only after I've decided, then we can put together a final budget and plan.

(It was decided that, for the purposes of the role play, the Collaborator should submit a 'hypothetical' plan in order to continue the role play, so that something could be brought to his boss).

C: I have put together a plan. Would you like me to show it to you? (The Collaborator attempts to move next to the Chief of Production.)

CP: (Grabs the plan from the Collaborator's hands) Thank you...(looks at plan)...I have a remark....wide...articulated and in depth....but it seems out of proportion in relation to the goal.

C: Could you be more precise? You said wide?

CP: Let me tell you in two words: Waste $100,000, Plan $300,000. If this plan is just related to avoiding waste I would be paying three years to recover it.

I must admit that it is interesting long term...but this wouldn't be for a problem of waste but a company policy problem. I must go to your boss.

This plan presupposes the factory will have life for years to come and that they want to have it.

C: Let me say something. Given that we want to evaluate this with my boss and find a solution that is shared, it might be useful to harmonize our functions. Let's go to this meeting with some solutions. We might reduce some of the cost by not training everybody, but just training some.

CP: I understand it is important to find a shared solution, but are you suggesting that this plan can be reduced and still fit my goal? I expected a well targeted plan. I must think there are some goals included other than what I asked for.

C: I am only suggesting we should try to balance effectiveness with budget...we might find a solution.

CP: I keep not understanding. It seems you took the opportunity to do something more with this plan than was needed. Why should I reduce effectiveness? I asked for the minimum to produce effectiveness. Let's go to your boss.

PHASE III (Chief of Production, Director of Personnel and collaborator meet in one room)

Collaborator: (Tries to sit next to his boss) Shall I sit here?

Director of Personnel: What are you doing? Sit there (across from the Chief of Production).

Chief of Production: Your collaborator came to me and submitted a plan that goes beyond my budget. I can't afford it in relation to the short term goal.

DP: Excuse me. I haven't had a chance to talk with my collaborator about this. Which plan was it?

C: The plan was for the workers' leaders relating to managing human resources, leadership skills and management skills.

DP: (To Collaborator) Did any new courses come out of this?

C: No, it confirmed our first impression.

CP: Everything is right...beautiful...but I had $100,000 waste and a plan that costs three times that much. He is saying it is an organizational plan that enables the 'factory of the future'. Is it going to survive? If it is worth the cost and design, then we've got to find the money, but not all from my pocket.

DP: It is worth it because we have to stabilize.

   You were referring to the problem of money and it is obvious that this hasn't been coded in terms of budget. At the moment we decide to implement it we'll have to find the financial coverage which goes beyond - we'll have to fund it out of the budget or find other terms.

   As far as your goals are concerned, this might slow you down because we still have to pull people out for training. But, in the medium term, do you think this plan is able to address your problems?

CP: If my goal is just limiting defective material this is not congruent - too much time, people, cost. But if we shift from waste to training...

DP: Let's make another distinction; waste is only one side - absenteeism is another. We think that training motivates people because they feel they are more a part of the company.

CP: Yes, but I then I want the plan to be considered part of company policy and the budget covered somewhere else.

END OF ROLE PLAY

After the role play, the "Director of Personnel" commented to the group that, although the Collaborator did as well as could be expected, he was confirmed in his concern that the Collaborator said, "Perfect," too quickly. Upon reflection, it was decided that the comment was more of a "meta message" about the desire of the Collaborator to appear competent, and to please his boss, than it was a message that the Collaborator fully understood the 'problem space' of the situation (i.e., it was more of a meta message at the level of "who", than it was about the clarity of the "what" and "how." These observations brought up a discussion about the importance of being able to distinguish such cues, and to better understand the perspectives and intentions of others.

The "Director of Personnel" also commented that it was important that he stay focused on the needs and problems of the Chief of Production, and not appear to be critical of the Collaborator. He explained that he had instructed his Collaborator to sit across from the Chief of Production rather than next to him, so that the Collaborator would be able to better observe and model the way that he (the Director of Personnel) handled the situation (whether the Collaborator was aware that this was happening or not). This lead to a discussion of the relevance of physical positioning (or "psychogeography") in training on the job, and in other leadership situations.

Patterns and Results

The fundamental goal of Training on the job is "activating people in a system." The process of training on the job can be divided into two basic phases; 1) initial training, and 2) training over time.

Initial job training goals involve the transfer of information for the purpose of managing problems; i.e., 1) knowledge, 2) attitude, 3) methods and 4) technical support.

Goals for job training over time include professional growth and the widening of discretionary space for the collaborator in regard to:

1) managing situations
2) internalizing concepts
3) using tools and instruments in an innovative way
4) accomplishing a shared objective with another person who is coming from a different starting point

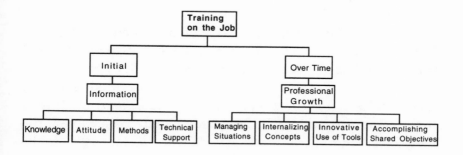

**Training on the Job Involves both Providing
Information and Supporting Professional Growth**

The key "operations" relating to the leadership skills that accompany training on the job, are those relating to the delegation of goals, and the criteria defining the successful achievement of those goals. Goals are typically the most tangible expressions of values. The goal "to increase profitability," for instance, clearly presupposes a valuing of "profit." The goal "to reach a consensus," on the other hand, obviously places value on "consensus."

In many ways, training on the job involves teaching, or showing, people how to manifest or enact key values within widely differing contexts. Values such as "quality," "acknowledgments," "cooperation," etc., do not show up the same way in different contexts and circumstances. Training on the job often involves making the meaning of such value statements explicit ("denominalizing" them) through particular reference experiences.

Some of the main ways that leaders communicate and teach values are:

1. What leaders pay attention to through time.
2. Leaders' reactions to critical events.
3. Role modeling the behaviors associated with values in different situations.

These are all forms of what can be called "Messenger-Message Congruency." One of the leader's primary ways of influencing his or her collaborators is to teach by example (to "walk" his or her "talk"). It has been pointed out that "communication is short term learning," and "learning is long term communication." To be trusted and "believable," the messages, and meta messages, of the leader need to be congruent with as many different aspects of the ongoing context as possible. What the leader communicates must be congruent with the organizational culture, his or her 'status' in the organization, the level of emphasis (identity, beliefs, values, capabilities, behaviors, etc.), his or internal state, company objectives, etc. Wherever there is a perceived incongruency, the leader loses credibility.

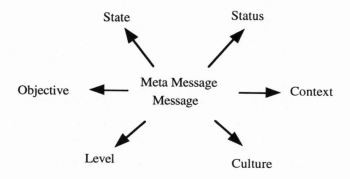

Reference Points for Messenger-Message Congruency

Summary of Key Leadership Skills:

Overall, leadership ability with respect to training on the job involves developing the capabilities to:

- Be congruent and coherent with "reality" (i.e., not overly idealistic or negative). One must connect "leadership" with ongoing context - content, problem situations, values, etc.

- Be comprehensible and clear - a good communicator.

- Promote consensus.

- Manage "power" - i.e., Know how to take it, leverage it, and utilize it.

- Construct and maintain a more global map of the situation.

- Increase his or her speed of thinking. This involves creativity and imagining solutions in a tempo faster than other people. This also involves the ability to convince people to accept this speed so that they are willing to test solutions.

- Simplify situations. Forming a more global map, and increasing thinking speed, involves the ability to simplify.

- Make everybody feel that they are significant, relevant, growing, and that they exist; i.e., valuing collaborators and having them sense that you value them.

- Maintain conviction - It is different "selling" ideas or behaviors than "believing" in them.

- "Feed needs" - People have different needs: professional, situational, individual. "To be effective through time people need to get something out of it." Leadership involves being aware of the evolution of the needs of the individual. "To guarantee a long term relationship you must invest."

- Stay aware of and manage one's relationship with one's own leader.

These abilities could be summarized as the following "Seven C's of Leadership":

1) Conviction
2) Consensus - Commitment
3) Clarity
4) Communication
5) Consistency
6) Congruence
7) Creativity

Basic Perceptual Positions in Communication and Relationships

Many of the managers participating in the study mentioned that it was important for a leader to understand the characteristics of his or her collaborators by somehow entering their viewpoint or "feeling space." A number of leaders pointed out that "You cannot lead someone that you don't understand. You may be able to command, coerce, bribe, cajole or push them; but you cannot lead them unless you have some sense of who they are."

One key way to understand people better when you are interacting with them is to 'put yourself in their shoes'. This serves to shift your "perceptual position" with respect to the situation.

Certainly, our perceptions of situations and experiences are greatly influenced by the point of view or perspective from which we consider them. In addition to being in the shoes of another person, there are several basic "perceptual positions" from which an interaction may be viewed. Perceptual positions refer to the fundamental points of view one can take concerning the relationship between oneself and another person:

1st Position: Associated in your own point of view, beliefs and assumptions, seeing the external world through your own eyes - an "I" position.

2nd Position: Associated in another person's point of view, beliefs and assumptions, seeing the external world through his or her eyes - a "you" position.

3rd Position: Associated in a point of view outside of the relationship between yourself and the other person - a "they" position.

4th Position: Associated in the perspective of the whole system - a "we" position. This is what one leader described as a "thinking vision of the system."

As the descriptions above indicate, perceptual positions are characterized and expressed by key words - "I," "you," "they," and "we." In a way, these key words are a type of meta message that can help you to recognize and direct the perceptual positions people are assuming during a particular interaction. For instance, someone who frequently uses the word "I" is more likely to be speaking from his or her point of view than a person who is using the word "we" when talking about ideas or suggestions. A person who is stuck in one perspective can be paced and lead to shift perceptual positions through the subtle use of such language cues.

For example, let's say a member of a project team is being overly critical of an idea or plan and says something like, "I don't think this will ever work", indicating a strong 'first position' reaction. The leader could help to verbally "lead" the individual to a more 'systemic' position by saying, "I understand you have some big concerns about this plan. How do you think we can approach it in a way that will work?"

To guide the person to an observer position, the leader could suggest, "Imagine you were a consultant for this team. What ways would you suggest for us to work together more effectively?" To encourage the critical individual to go to 'second position' the leader could say, "Put yourself in my shoes (or one of the other team members) for a moment. What reactions do you think I would have to your concern?"

Certainly, one of the most important communication and relational skills a leader can develop for himself or herself is the ability to switch points of view and take multiple perspectives of a situation or experience.

Psychogeography

"Psychogeography" refers to the influence that micro-geographical arrangements and relationships exert on people's psychological processes and interpersonal interactions. The term 'psychogeography' is drawn from the field of psychodrama and the work of J. Moreno. The author introduced the term into NLP in the mid 1980's as part of his work involving the use of spatial sorting in NLP techniques.

"Psychogeography" relates to the fact that the geographical relationship between the members of a group has an important non-verbal influence upon the group's process and interactions with one another. The spatial relationships and orientation between people exerts both a physical and symbolic influence on the interaction between group members. Psychogeography creates a type of relational "circuitry" between people, determining the type and quality of interaction.

Consider the simplest case of two individuals interacting with one another. If they stand face to face at a close distance, this psychogeography will create and support a direct, and likely intense, interaction between the two of them (either positive or negative). If the two move farther away from one another, the intensity of the interaction is likely to diminish. If the two stand side by side, the essential nature of their relationship and interaction will most likely shift a bit. They become more like partners or members of a team, focused on a common direction or task rather than on each other. If one person stands slightly behind and to the side of the other, he or she will most likely begin to enter the role of a supporter or mentor to the other.

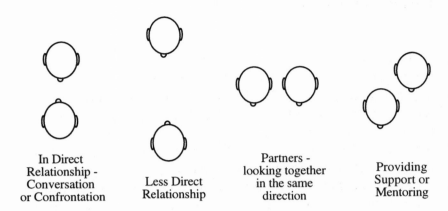

In Direct
Relationship -
Conversation
or Confrontation

Less Direct
Relationship

Partners -
looking together
in the same
direction

Providing
Support or
Mentoring

**"Psychogeography" Influences and Expresses
the Quality of Relationship and Interaction Between
People.**

The same types of arrangements of "circuitry" influence, and are reflected in, the behavior of larger groups. Consider the constellation or "circuit" represented by the interaction below. A lot can be inferred about the quality of the interaction and the relationships between the various individuals involved by their psychogeography.

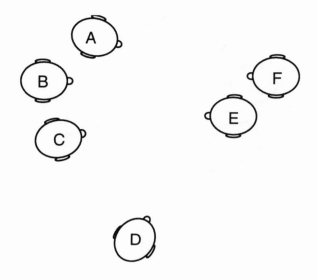

The Psychogeography of a Group Reflects Their Relationships and Interactions with One Another

It seems evident that A, B and C make up one group, E and F make up another group, and D seems to be more of an observer. The attention of all the group members, however, appears to be mostly focused on E. E appears to have more of a leadership role with F as a supporter. A, B and C, on the other hand, seem to be more equal in status.

Notice the difference between the previous grouping and the following grouping, in which F has changed location.

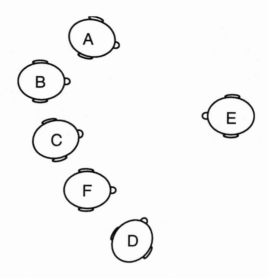

Different Psychogeographies Reflect and Reinforce Different Interactions and Relationships

In this arrangement, all of the individuals appear to be one group, with E directing or leading the group in some way. The attention of F, however, appears to be directed somewhere other than on E.

Psychogeography has important implications for leadership and group dynamics. Setting up a meeting room in a certain way, for instance, is a "meta message" about the kind of interaction that people are expected to engage in. As an example, sitting in a circle, as in a round table, encourages different types of feedback and interactions between group members than sitting at a rectangular table, or in a 'theater style' arrangement. A round table also conveys a different kind of symbolic relationship between group members. For example, if someone enters a room that is set up with a blackboard at the front and chairs arranged facing the front of the room in "theater style," he or she is likely to interpret it as a context for a 'presentation' and be prepared to sit passively and listen. If that person enters a room in which a small group of chairs is arranged facing each other in a "round table" format, he or she will most likely interpret it as a context for 'discussion' and be ready to be more proactive and participative.

A circular psychogeography will tend to focus people on their interpersonal relationships, distributing attention equally between all group members and implying an equal status between them all. Sitting around a rectangular table, on the other hand, creates a sense of hierarchy. Focus is typically directed toward the head of the table, and the person sitting at the "head of the table" is usually the person with highest status, followed by the person sitting closest to his or her "right hand" side, and then the "left hand".

Sitting in a semi-circle would tend to focus the attention of the group members toward whatever is at the front of the semi-circle. It tends to imply equality of status among the individuals in the semi-circle, working to take action or reach a consensus with respect to whatever is at the center of their common focus. A group sitting side-by-side in a straight line, would also imply a common focus for all group members, but would greatly reduce the interaction between members with one another. They would be acting but not 'interacting' as a group.

Different psychogeographies can be constructed and utilized to promote different types of group processes. A circle, for instance, is an effective psychogeography for "dreaming" or brainstorming because it intensifies the interaction between group members. It implies that all members, and thus all ideas, are of equal value, and people can "bounce" ideas off one another rapidly, and quickly add to the ideas of others, without becoming overly focused on any one individual or idea.

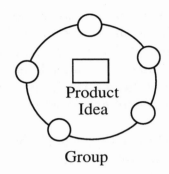

Effective "Psychogeography" for "Dreaming" or Brainstorming

A semi-circle is a more effective psychogeography for "realizing," or planning how to implement a particular goal or dream. In a semi-circle, people would be still considered peers, but their focus is much more directed toward a particular point. The idea or plan has become disconnected from any particular group member, and is the common focus of everyone in the group. The implication is that the group is much more focused on their task than their relationship, and that they are moving toward consensus.

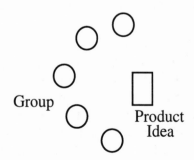

Effective "Psychogeography" for "Realizing" or Planning

A psychogeography in which the group members are all in a line, sitting next to one another, as if they were a panel, looking at the goal or idea, is a more effective psychogeography for criticizing or evaluating. While their proximity to one another presupposes that each person is part of the same group. Individuals, however, will be much more inclined to respond in accordance with their own perspective, as opposed to checking out the reactions of other group members.

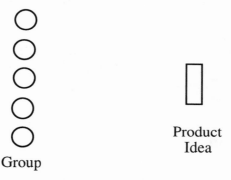

Group   Product
Idea

Effective "Psychogeography" for Criticizing or Evaluating

Applications and Tools

The following exercises provide a way to practice some of the key cognitive, interactive and linguistic skills of leadership in the context of training on the job. The exercises involve preparing for challenging situations, involving significant others, applying multiple perceptual positions and the awareness of psychogeography, along with various aspects of the Communication Matrix, in order to anticipate and prepare oneself to respond in the most appropriate and congruent way.

The purpose of the exercises is to develop the skills necessary to form a "more global map" of situations requiring leadership, and to "think ahead" more quickly and effectively.

The Meta Map

The Meta Map is a process developed by the author in the late 1980's as a means to map and effectively intervene in challenging interactions, situations and relationships. The Meta Map is an extension of the Meta Mirror technique (Dilts, 1990, 1992), which was formulated by the author as a result of applying the concept of Perceptual Positions (DeLozier & Grinder, 1987) to interpersonal communication. In addition to Perceptual Positions, the Meta Map involves the use of Psychogeography, Characterological Adjectives, Systemic Thinking, and the various distinctions of the Communication Matrix.

The purpose of the Meta Map is to assist a person to identify and then alter characteristics of the communication loops that are producing or maintaining a problematic interaction. Often, when we experience difficulties in communicating with others, we become entrenched in our own point of view. The Meta Map begins by acknowledging that perspective, but then provides us with the opportunity to see the interaction from other points of view. In addition to identifying "invisible" (i.e., internal and non-physical) influences on the situation, the Meta Map allows us to see and modify some of the ways in which we may be contributing to our own difficulties.

The basic steps of the Meta Map include: (a) identifying a difficult or challenging communication situation; (b) mapping the dynamics occurring between oneself, the other person in the interaction, and one's inner observer; (c) taking the perspective of the other person, and viewing the situation from his or her point of view; (d) establishing a "meta position" from which to examine both mental and physical patterns occurring within the interaction that may be contributing to the problem; and (e) exploring possible changes in communication, attitude or assumptions that could make the interaction more comfortable and productive.

In addition to providing a useful strategy for reflecting on or preparing for a difficult meeting or interaction, the Meta Map can be used as a coaching or consulting technique. There are several variations of the Meta Map, depending on the type of situation to which it is being applied. The following is a way to apply the Meta Map to a challenging communication situation.

Making a Meta Map for Leadership

One of the most intriguing aspects of this part of the leadership study occurred during the enactment of the three-phase role plays; but it did not occur during the actual role play. It relates to the time that the individuals who were the assigned "leaders" in the role play had to wait outside the room, while their "collaborators" were enacting the second part of the role play. The "leader" knew that he or she would be coming back into a challenging, and largely unpredictable, interactive situation. Following the role plays, the individuals who had been in the "leader" position were asked about how they prepared themselves mentally to meet the challenges. A common response was:

I would think about the people involved in the situation, and imagine the possible actions they could take that would create problems. I would then look at myself and try to see what I could do in response, and whether I felt comfortable with that. I also tried to see the situation from the other person's perspective, and get a sense of what motives might be behind their actions. I would then view the situation from the company's perspective to see what was going to be the best way to handle the situation for all concerned. Having done my 'homework', I would finally think about what internal state I wanted to be in, and what state would help me respond most creatively and appropriately. I figured that if I was in the wrong state, I wouldn't be able to respond well no matter what happened; but if I was in the right state, the inspiration would be there, even if something happened that I hadn't prepared for.

The following is a variation of the Meta Map, based on the strategies of effective leaders, that can be applied as a strategy for reflecting on, or planning for, a challenging leadership situation.

For each of the significant people/roles in the interaction, map out the problem space and solution space by going through the following steps:

A. Define the Problem Space.

1. Imagine that the person is in front of you right now, interacting with you. Imagine the range of possible behaviors that could create problems.

2. Take an observer point of view with regard to the interaction, perceiving it as if you were seeing it from the point of view of someone outside of the relationship ('Company Position'). Picture your own behavior in response to the other person, and evaluate your state and status (e.g., a frustrated "boss" and nervous "collaborator").

   a. Is the relationship symmetrical, complementary or reciprocal?

   b. What is the state or attitude of the other person and of yourself in relation to the other person? Are they polarized? On the same level? Matched?

   c. Is it a stable, escalating or deescalating system? Does the way you are acting actually reinforce or trigger the behavior of the other person in the system?

3. Now take a step to the side and look at how you treat yourself in this interaction. What is your outcome for the interaction? Is there a congruency between the 'professional' you and the 'personal' you?

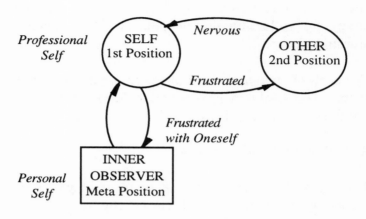

Making a 'Meta Map' involves Checking Your Personal and Professional Congruency

    a. How does your inner congruence (or lack of congru-ence) effect the total system of communication? If you changed your response to yourself, would it effect the interaction?

    b. If you are not congruent, what would it take to align your personal and professional identities?

4. Now put yourself inside the other person's role - imagine you were "in that person's shoes". How do you experi-ence your own behavior from that perspective?

    a. Are there any other influences on this person from outside of the physical sphere of the interaction that you notice and need to add to the map?

    b. If you were in this other person's world view, what would be your intention in this interaction?

5. Go back to the observer perspective and consider that if the problematic behaviors in this interaction were just a symptom what would be the cause(s)?

   a. Sort out the messages from the meta messages in the communication. Are the intended messages being received? If not, what messages *are* being received?

   b. Notice at which logical levels (behavior, capability, belief, identity) the different responses are operating.

   c. What thinking styles (Dreamer, Realist, Critic) are operating?

   d. How does your physical location (psychogeography) influence the way the communication is being interpreted?

   e. Where is the uncertainty in the system? Identity? Role? Policy? Values? Procedures? Path? Goals? Context?

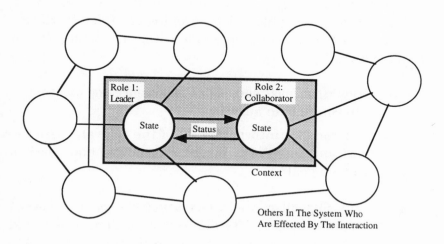

A 'Meta Map' Identifies as Much of the Problem Space of the Interaction as Possible

B. Broaden your Solution Space as much as Possible.

1. Approaching the problem space from the criteria of leadership, what is the most appropriate long term result for this interaction from the company position?

   1) Conviction
   2) Consensus
   3) Clarity
   4) Communication
   5) Consistency
   6) Congruence
   7) Creativity

2. As a leader, what resources do you have that would address the whole problem space in order to better achieve this result?

3. Imagine how you might make the appropriate alterations to messages, meta messages, logical levels, meta programs, and physical positioning in order to clarify, align or balance the interaction within the total solution space.

   a. Draw upon past successful experiences or mentors to help you find an answer.

   b. How can you incorporate all of the relevant perspectives and intentions in order to define and reach a common goal?

4. Considering all of the information you have gathered about the situation, determine what *internal state* would help you to respond most resourcefully and appropriately, and get into that state as fully as possible.

5. Put yourself back into your own first position with respect to your interaction with the other person. Notice how your reactions and point of view have changed.

6. Put yourself into the other person's perspective (second position) and notice what change in response you experience from that viewpoint with respect to the interaction.

7. Keep changing your perceptual position, logical level, meta program patterns and psychogeography within the solution space until you have arrived at and future paced a new solution to the original problem.

Leadership Simulation/Role Play Exercise

The following exercise involves defining a challenging leadership situation and then using a mix of leadership skills to explore new solutions.

Start by identifying a challenging situation in which you would like to strengthen or improve your ability to lead or influence another person or group in a positive way.

1. Pair up with another person, who will act as your 'coach'. Define the 'problem space' of the situation by exploring the questions below.

   a. What is the external context of the situation?

   Is the context part of what makes the situation challenging? If so, can you change the context, or what can you do to reduce the impact of the context on your interaction?

   b. Who is the other person? What is that person's role or relationship with respect to you in this context?

   Is your role or relationship with the other person clear to both of you? Do you both have the same perception of your role or relationship? Is the perception of your role or relationship part of what makes the situation challenging? If so, in what ways can you alter or clarify the perception of your role or relationship, or what can you do to reduce the impact of the role or relationship on your interaction?

   c. What is the understood purpose of the interaction?

*Is the purpose of the interaction clear to both of
you? Is the perception of the purpose of the
interaction part of what makes the situation
challenging? If so, in what ways can you alter or
clarify the perception of the purpose of the
interaction?*

d. What are the key characteristics of the other person? (If
there is more than one person, choose a representative
member of the group to explore; i.e., a person, or
composite person, who symbolizes or typifies the group.)
Create a location representing the position of the other
person and go to "second position" by physically putting
yourself into the "shoes" of that person. Identify key
characteristics of that person's internal state, physical
behaviors, cognitive patterns, and beliefs and values.

Internal State   Key Behaviors

Cognitive Style   Values & Beliefs
(Dreamer, Realist, Critic, etc.)

*Which of the key characteristics of the other person
makes the situation challenging? What could be
the positive intention behind those particular
characteristics? What might help to shift or redirect
those characteristics? What leadership style, or
combination of styles) have you already attempted
to use with this person? What stopped it from
being effective?*

e. Given the information that you have defined above, what is your outcome with respect to yourself in this situation? What internal state do you want to maintain, regardless of what the other person does?

What will be your evidence that you have achieved this outcome? What specific cues in your posture, gestures, voice tone, feelings, etc., will let you know that you are achieving your desired state?

f. What is your outcome for the other person in this situation? (Think of the person's internal state and thinking processes as well as his or her behavior.)

What will be your evidence that you have achieved this outcome with respect to the other person?

Also consider:
What is the other person's outcome for himself or herself?

What is his or her outcome for you?

2. Get together with another pair to form a group of four: a 'leader', his or her coach, a role player and an observer/meta person. The leader and role player will simulate a 'leadership' interaction while the others observe.

3. The goal of the 'leader' is to use his or her verbal and non-verbal communication abilities, and his or her knowledge of the other person, in order to widen the perceptual space of the role player, and attempt to reach the outcomes for the situation. Enact the simulation for 10 minutes.

Some communication skills to be used by the leader include:

Backtracking

Rephrasing objections and criticisms into 'how' questions

Identifying positive intentions

Chunking up to find common criteria

Clarifying perceptual positions, time frames and logical levels

4. Following the role play, the whole group is to then go to an "observer position" and discuss which of the skills were utilized effectively by the leader. Group members are to state what they liked about the leader's skills and suggest something the leader might do more of, or do differently. (10 minutes maximum)

Chapter 9

Conclusion

The Fiat leadership project was successful in a number of ways. In addition to identifying important capabilities that were incorporated into Fiat's training seminars on leadership, many of the skills that were modeled in the study became part of Fiat's basic training program for their managers.

As a result of these contributions, two further experimental seminars on other aspects of leadership were organized. In November 1990 a second modeling seminar, focusing on systemic thinking skills, was conducted with the same leaders who had participated in the initial project. The purpose of this program was to identify specific systemic thinking skills and strategies applied by effective managers in relationship to concrete and dynamic leadership situations. Research included identifying the types of mental maps, assumptions and questions leaders used in order achieve outcomes and solve problems in situations involving a high degree of complexity and uncertainty.

In November 1991, a third modeling seminar focusing on the management of beliefs and values was conducted. The purpose of this study was to apply the tools of NLP to examine the specific skills used by effective leaders to manage beliefs and values. In particular, it focused on issues arising with respect to collaborators, groups and teams in challenging leadership situations involving the accomplishment of a specific job or task.

The results of these studies were both fascinating and valuable, but beyond the scope of this book. Some of the patterns discovered during these programs appear in *Visionary Leadership Skills*. The rest, however, will have to wait for future volumes.

Fiat has successfully made it through the "changing of the guard," and it has been rewarding to see many of the younger managers that participated in the experimental modeling seminars move into more senior positions. I have continued to have an active involvement in other projects with Fiat over the past decade, and am presently an associate professor for the ISVOR Fiat School of Management.

The field of NLP has also evolved tremendously over the past two decades; primarily as a result of the continued application of modeling in many new areas. These developments are best exemplified by the NLP Community Leadership Project. In June of 1997, 190 NLP trainers, developers, authors and founders of NLP institutes gathered in Santa Cruz, California, in order to gaze into the future together for the purpose of:

- Creating a positive vision of the future and the role that NLP plays in that future.

- Defining ways in which NLP can contribute to the communities and systems of which we are members.

- Formulating specific projects and plans that will lead to that future.

The event was co-facilitated by myself, Judith DeLozier and Teresa Epstein, of NLP University; Tim Hallbom and Suzi Smith, of Anchor Point Productions; and Lara Ewing, of NLP Comprehensive. There were a total of twenty three project groups, encompassing many areas that will shape our lives, including:

Environment	Health
Communications and Networking	
Family and Community	Research
Inter-Cultural Relations	Epistemology and Modeling
Media	Human Rights
Technology	Education
Business Management	Leadership
Politics	Arts and Creativity

Each group produced a vision statement and a plan for implementation that were collected into a booklet comprising over a hundred pages, which is being published and made available to NLP practitioners and institutes throughout the world. An Internet web site, including information on the NLP Community Leadership Project plans and participants has been established at: http://nlpu.com. This creates the opportunity for anyone who is interested to participate in creating our future, and the future of NLP.

The spirit of creativity and cooperation, and the unselfish commitment of the NLP Community Leadership Project participants to contribute to the larger community, was truly an inspiration for the future possibilities of NLP. Future meetings of the NLP Community Leadership project are planned for the year 2000 and will continue on into the next millenium.

For more information on the NLP Community Leadership Project and seminars on NLP, Modeling and Leadership please contact:

NLP University
P.O. Box 1112
Ben Lomond, California 95005
Phone: (408) 336-3457
Fax: (408) 336-5854
http://nlpu.com

Afterword

I hope you have enjoyed this exploration into *Modeling With NLP*. If you are interested in exploring modeling or leadership in more depth, other tools and resources exist to further develop and apply the models, strategies and skills described within these pages.

NLP University is an organization committed to providing the highest quality trainings in basic and advanced NLP skills, and to promoting the development of new models and applications of NLP in the areas of health, business and organization, creativity and learning. Each Summer, NLP University holds residential programs at the University of California at Santa Cruz, offering extended residential courses on the skills of both modeling and leadership.

For more information please contact:

NLP University
P.O. Box 1112
Ben Lomond, California 95005
Phone: (408) 336-3457
Fax: (408) 336-5854
http://nlpu.com

Systemic Solutions International is a training and consulting company established in order to help businesses and organizations define and achieve desired states through the use of NLP based tools and methods. Its mission is to provide the materials and the support necessary to promote effective and ecological change in social systems. The core of Systemic Solutions International is a set of engineered materials for people in medium to large organizations, developed through research projects and training interventions conducted with companies such as Fiat, IBM, Apple Computer, Lucasfilms and the State Railway in Italy. A key feature of the SSI product line is its unique approach to systemic change which involves a combination of seminars, self learning paths and assisted learning paths.

For more information about the specific products and services provided by Systemic Solutions International, please contact the address below.

Systemic Solutions
International

343 Soquel Ave., #149
Santa Cruz, CA 95062
Tel: (408) 662-6685
Fax: (408) 426-8345

The *Global NLP Training and Consulting Community* (GTC) was established to provide skilled NLP practitioners and developers with further opportunities to network and collaborate. The vision of the GTC is that of a worldwide network of competent trainers, consultants, developers and sponsors who share the mission of bringing the presuppositions and practices of NLP to social systems, organizations, groups and individuals. This is being accomplished through the establishment of a unique training path covering key skills required for consulting and training, such as presenting, coaching, instructional design, information gathering, problem solving, assessment and practice management. The structure of the Global NLP Training and Consulting Community is designed to offer support and networking opportunities to members, such as the establishment of an international referral network. It includes an Internet web site and an international directory of members who have completed the certification path at:

http://nlpu.com/GTC.htm

Appendix A: The R.O.L.E. Model

The term R.O.L.E. Model was coined by Robert Dilts in 1987 to describe the four basic NLP elements involved in modeling cognitive strategies. The goal of the R.O.L.E. modeling process is to identify the essential elements of thinking and behavior used to produce a particular response or outcome. This involves identifying the critical steps of the mental strategy and the role each step plays in the overall neurological "program". This role is determined by the following four factors which are indicated by the letters which make up the name of the **R.O.L.E.** Model - *Representational systems; Orientation; Links; Effect.*

Representational Systems have to do with which of the five senses are most dominant for the particular mental step in the strategy: **V**isual (sight), **A**uditory (sound), **K**inesthetic (feeling), **O**lfactory (smell), **G**ustatory (taste).

Each representational system is designed to perceive certain basic qualities of the experiences it senses. These include characteristics such as *color, brightness, tone, loudness, temperature, pressure,* etc. These qualities are called "sub-modalities" in NLP since they are sub-components of each of the representational systems.

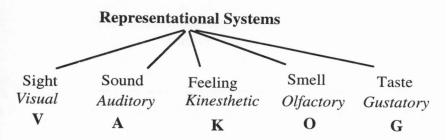

Representational Systems

Sight	Sound	Feeling	Smell	Taste
Visual	*Auditory*	*Kinesthetic*	*Olfactory*	*Gustatory*
V	**A**	**K**	**O**	**G**

Our Representational Systems Relate to Our Five Senses

Orientation has to do with whether a particular sensory representation is focused (**e**)xternally toward the outside world or (**i**)nternally toward either (**r**)emembered or (**c**)onstructed experiences. For instance, when you are seeing something, is it in the outside world, in your memory, or in your imagination?

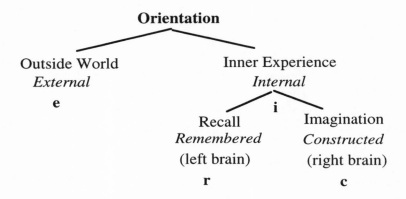

Orientation

Outside World
External
e

Inner Experience
Internal
i

Recall
Remembered
(left brain)
r

Imagination
Constructed
(right brain)
c

Links have to do with how a particular step or sensory representation is linked to the other representations. For example, is something seen in the external environment linked to internal feelings, remembered images, words? Is a particular feeling linked to constructed pictures, memories of sounds or other feelings?

There are two basic ways that representations can be linked together: sequentially and simultaneously. Sequential links act as *anchors* or triggers such that one representation follows another in a linear chain of events.

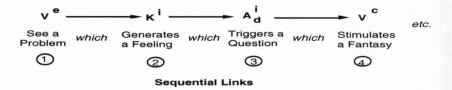

V^e ⟶ K^i ⟶ A^i_d ⟶ V^c *etc.*

See a Problem   *which*   Generates a Feeling   *which*   Triggers a Question   *which*   Stimulates a Fantasy

①   ②   ③   ④

Sequential Links

Simultaneous links occur as what are called *synesthesias.* Synesthesia links have to do with the ongoing overlap between sensory representations. Certain qualities of feelings may be linked to certain qualities of imagery - for example, visualizing the shape of a sound or hearing a color.

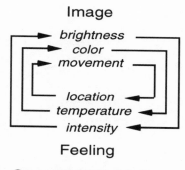

Synesthesia Links

Certainly, both of these kinds of links are essential to thinking, learning, creativity and the general organization of our experiences.

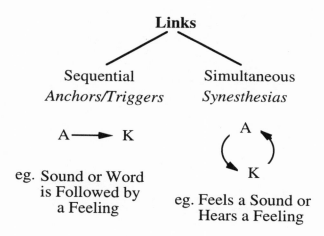

Effect has to do with the result, effect or purpose of each step in the thought process. For instance, the function of the step could be to generate or input a sensory representation, to test or evaluate a particular sensory representation or to operate to change some part of an experience or behavior in relationship to a sensory representation.

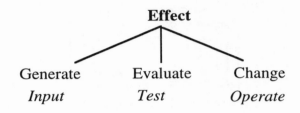

Physiological Clues: Making the R.O.L.E. into a B.A.G.E.L.

The R.O.L.E. model elements deal primarily with cognitive processes. In order to function, however, these mental programs need the help of certain bodily and physiological processes for consolidation and expression. These physical reactions are important for the teaching or development of certain mental processes as well as for the external observation and confirmation of them. The primary behavioral elements involved in R.O.L.E. modeling are:

Body Posture.
Accessing cues
Gestures.
Eye movements.
Language Patterns.

1. **B**ody Posture

People often assume systematic, habitual postures when deep in thought. These postures can indicate a great deal about the representational system the person is using. The following are some typical examples:

a. Visual: *Leaning back with head and shoulders up or rounded, shallow breathing.*

b. Auditory: *Body leaning forward, head cocked, shoulders back, arms folded.*

c. Kinesthetic: *Head and shoulders down, deep breathing.*

2. Accessing Cues

When people are thinking, they cue or trigger certain types of representations in a number of different ways including: breathing rate, non-verbal "grunts and groans", facial expressions, snapping their fingers, scratching their heads, and so on. Some of these are idiosyncratic to the individual and need to be 'calibrated' to the particular person. Many of these cues, however, are associated to particular sensory processes"

  a. Visual: High shallow breathing, squinting eyes, higher voice pitch, and faster tempo.
  b. Auditory: Diaphragmatic breathing, knitted brow, fluctuating voice tone and tempo.
  c. Kinesthetic: Deep abdominal breathing, deep breathy voice in a slower tempo.

3. Gestures.

People will often touch, point to or use gestures indicating the sense organ they are using to think with. Some typical examples include:

  a. Visual: *Touching or pointing to the eyes; gestures made above eye level.*
  b. Auditory: *Pointing toward or gesturing near the ears; touching the mouth or jaw.*
  c. Kinesthetic: *Touching the chest and stomach area; gestures made below the neck.*

4. Eye movements

Automatic, unconscious eye movements often accompany particular thought processes indicating the accessing of one of the representational systems. NLP has categorized these cues into the following pattern:

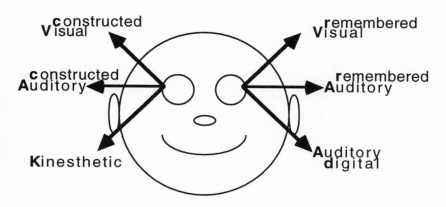

NLP Eye Movement Chart

5. Language Patterns

A primary method of Neuro-Linguistic analysis is to search for particular linguistic patterns, such as 'predicates', which indicate a particular neurological representational system or sub-modality, and how that system or quality is being used in the overall program of thought. Predicates are words, such as verbs, adverbs and adjectives, which indicate actions or qualities as opposed to things. This type of language is typically selected at an unconscious level and thus reflects the underlying unconscious structure which produced them. Below is a list of common sensory based predicates:

VISUAL	**AUDITORY**	**KINESTHETIC**
"see"	"hear"	"grasp"
"look"	"listen"	"touch"
"sight"	"sound"	"feeling"
"clear"	"resonant"	"solid"
"bright"	"loud"	"heavy"
"picture"	"word"	"handle"
"hazy"	'noisy'	"rough"
"brings to light"	"rings a bell"	"connects"
"show"	"tell"	"move

Appendix B:
Meta Program Patterns

Meta Programs emerged as a part of NLP in the late 1970's. A number of the patterns were initially proposed by Richard Bandler as ways in which people kept "coherency" in their mental programming (like the reference beam in an optical hologram). Further research into these and other patterns was spearheaded by Leslie Cameron-Bandler (together with David Gordon, Robert Dilts and Maribeth Meyers-Anderson). As the name implies, "meta" programs are about other programs. They are the programs which guide and direct other thought processes. Specifically, they define common or typical patterns in the strategies or thinking styles of a particular individual, group or culture.

Both Meta Program patterns and much of the current NLP Submodality technology came from the attempt to better understand the functioning of cognitive strategies. In particular, they developed as a way to explain how individuals with the same cognitive structure to their strategies could sometimes end up with widely divergent results. For instance, two people might share a decision strategy with the structure: Vc—>Ki (deriving feelings from constructed images as a way to make a decision).

One person, however, might report, "I picture several options, and choose the one that feels right to me." The other person, on the other hand, might complain, "I picture several options, and then feel overwhelmed and confused by them." The notion of Meta Programs arose from attempting to discover what made the difference between such diverse responses. Because the general representational structure of the strategies was essentially the same, it was postulated that the differences came from patterns outside of, or "meta to", the strategy (or internal program); i.e., a "Meta Program."

Meta Program patterns and Submodalities determine the qualities of, and relationships between, the experiences and information that is being represented in a particular cognitive strategy. They address characteristics relating to the experiential substance of a particular image, set of words or feeling state. They influence how experiences are represented, sorted and punctuated. They also direct where we place our attention, operating as another set of filters on our experience.

Meta Programs (in contrast with Submodalities) are more abstract than our specific strategies for thinking, and define our general approach to a particular issue rather than the details of our thinking process. Meta Program patterns are descriptions of the different ways in which a 'problem space', or elements of a problem space, may be approached.

As with other NLP distinctions, a person can apply the same Meta Program pattern regardless of the content and context of a situation. Also, they are not "all or nothing" distinctions and may occur together in varying proportions.

Overview of Meta Program Patterns

In approaching a problem or goal, one can emphasize moving *toward* something *positive*, *away from* something *negative*, or some combination of both. Approaching positives involves seeking to achieve desired visions, outcomes and dreams, and tends to foster entrepreneurship and 'proactivity'. Avoiding negatives involves attempting to circumvent potential mistakes and problems, and accompanies a more careful, conservative and 'reactive' approach to planning, decision making and problem solving. Those who exclusively 'move toward', however, can make decisions that are naive and potentially risky. Those who only 'move away' can seem overly pessimistic or "paranoid." Good decisions and plans generally involve some combination of both.

The Meta Program pattern of *chunk-size* relates to the level of specificity or generality with which a person or group is analyzing a problem or problem space. Situations may be analyzed in terms of varying degrees of *detail* (micro chunks of information) and *generalities* (macro chunks of information). Again, too much focus on details leads people to lose sight of the "big picture." Similarly, an overemphasis on generalities can compromise and weaken the ability to "follow through," because you can't see the discrete steps.

Goals or problem situations may be examined with reference to different *time frames*: i.e., long term, medium term or short term consequences. The time frame within which a problem or outcome is considered can greatly influence the way in which it is interpreted and approached. Placing too much emphasis on *short term* success, for instance, may lead to problems in long term ecology (i.e., one can "win the battle, but lose the war"). On the other hand, blindness to short term and *medium term* needs and challenges can threaten the success of *long term* goals ("the chain is no stronger than its weakest link").

Outcomes and problems can also be defined with reference to the *past, present* or *future*. Sometimes people are attempting to repeat successes or avoid problems that have recently occurred and are fresh in their minds. At other times people may seek to achieve or avoid more distant future outcomes or problems. Some people tend to look at history for solutions more so than the future. A good example is the difference between former Soviet leader Michail Gorbachev and the people who attempted to overthrow him before the dissolution of the Soviet Union in the early 1990's. One was trying to prepare for the future, while the others were trying to preserve the past.

Locus of control is another important Meta Program pattern. *Internal reference* is an NLP term used to describe the process by which a person uses his or her own inner feelings, representations and criteria as the primary source of his or her actions, and for evaluating the success of those actions. 'Internal reference' may be contrasted with *external reference*, in which the locus of control, or the evidence of success, with respect to a particular action or decision, is placed outside of the individual. Picking a job based on internal reference, for example, would involve determining one's own personal needs and desires, and selecting a position based on how well it matched those needs and interests. Choosing a job based on external reference would involve selecting one that pleased another person, or because it is the only position available. Thus, doing what one "wants" to do is more internally referenced. Doing what one "has to" do, or has been told one "should" do, is more externally referenced. Successful evidence and evidence procedures typically involve some combination of both internal and external references.

Success with respect to achieving a goal, or avoiding a problem, may be evaluated by either *matching* (sorting for similarities), or *mismatching* (seeking differences) between the current state and the goal state. Matching focuses attention on what has been achieved. Mismatching emphasizes what is missing. Matching tends to support the perception of unity and consensus, while mismatching can encourage diversity and innovation. Too much matching, however, can make a person seem insincere and easily swayed by the opinions of others. Too much mismatching makes a person seem disagreeable and overly critical.

Problems and outcomes may be considered in relation to the achievement of a *task*, or with respect to issues involving *relationship*, such as 'power' and 'affiliation.' Emphasis on task or relationship can be an important distinction for understanding differences in culture and gender. Men, for instance, are often considered to be more task oriented, while women are frequently seen as more attentive to relationships. The question of balance of focus with respect to task and relationship is often an essential one with respect to working with groups and teams. In the achievement of a task, either goals, procedures or options may be emphasized. (This in and of itself can lead to significant differences in a one's approach to problem solving or planning; a *procedure oriented* strategy will emphasize "doing it by the book," for instance, while an *options oriented* approach would involve finding as many variations as possible.) Issues involving relationship may be approached with an emphasis on the point of view of oneself, others or the larger system ('the company,' 'the market,' etc.) to varying degrees.

Strategies for approaching problems may emphasize various combinations of *vision, action, logic* or *emotion*. A particular emphasis on one of these cognitive strategies can produce a general *thinking style* at the level of a group or culture. Vision, action, logic and emotion are more general expressions of the elements of a particular cognitive strategy: i.e., visualization, movement, verbalization and feeling. Thinking style is akin to the NLP notion of "primary" or "most valued" representational system.

Summary of Key Meta Program Patterns

1. Approach To Problems
   a. Towards the Positive
   b. Away From the Negative

2. Time Frame:
   a. Short Term - Long Term
   b. Past - Present -Future

3. Chunk Size:
   a. Large Chunks - Generalities
   b. Small Chunks - Details

4. Locus of Control:
   a. Internal or 'Self' Reference - Proactive
   b. External or 'Other' Reference - Reactive

5. Mode of Comparison
   a. Match (Similarities) - Consensus
   b. Mismatch (Differences) - Confrontation

6. Approach to Problem Solving
   a. Task (Achievement)
      1) Choices - Goals
      2) Procedures - Operations

   b. Relationship (Power; Affiliation)
      1) Self - *My, I, Me*
      2) Other - *You, His, Their*
      3) Context - *We, The Company, The Market*

7. Thinking Style
   a. Vision
   b. Action
   c. Logic
   d. Emotion

Bibliography

Bagley, D., & Reese, E.; *Beyond Selling: How to Maximize Your Personal Influence;* Meta Publications, Capitola, CA, 1987.

Bandler, R. & Grinder J.; *The Structure of Magic, Volumes I & II;* Science and Behavior Books, Palo Alto, CA, 1975, 1976.

Bandler R. & Grinder J.; *Frogs into Princes;* Real People Press, Moab, UT, 1979.

Bass, B., *Leadership and Performance Beyond Expectations;* The Free Press, New York, NY, 1985.

Bass, Avolio & Goodheim, *Biography and the Assessment of Transformational Leadership at the World-Class Level;* Journal of Management, XIII, 1 March, 1987.

Bateson, G.; *Steps to an Ecology of Mind;* Ballantine Books, New York, NY, 1972.

Bateson, G.; *Mind and Nature;* E. P. Dutton, New York, NY, 1979.

Bennis, W. & Nanus, B; *Leaders: the Strategies for Taking Charge;* Harper and Row, New York, 1985.

Blanchard, K. & Johnson, S.; *The One Minute Manager;* Berkley Books, New York, NY, 1983.

Cameron-Bandler, L., Gordon, G. and Lebeau, M., *Know How*, Future Pace, San Rafael, CA, 1984.

Cameron-Bandler, L., Gordon, G. and Lebeau, M., *The Emprint Method*, Future Pace, San Rafael, CA, 1985.

Chomsky, N., *Syntactic Structures*, Mouton, The Hague, The Netherlands, 1957.

Chomsky, N., *Language and Mind*, Harcourt Brace Jovanovich, Inc., New York, NY, 1968.

DeLozier, J. & Grinder, J.; *Turtles All The Way Down*; Grinder, DeLozier & Associates, Santa Cruz, CA 1987.

Dilts, Grinder, Bandler & DeLozier; *Neuro-Linguistic Programming: The Study of the Structure of Subjective Experience, Vol. I;* Meta Publications, Capitola, CA, 1980.

Dilts R.; *Visionary Leadership Skills*; Meta Publications, Capitola, CA, 1996.

Dilts R.; *The Law of Requisite Variety*; NLP University Press, Ben Lomond, CA, 1998.

Dilts R.; *An Overview of Learning*; NLP University Press, Ben Lomond, CA, 1998.

Dilts R.; *Effective Presentation Skills*; Meta Publications, Capitola, CA, 1994.

Dilts R. with Bonissone, G.; *Skills for the Future: Managing Creativity and Innovation*; Meta Publications, Capitola, CA, 1993.

Dilts, R. B., Epstein, T. & Dilts, R. W.; *Tools for Dreamers: Strategies of Creativity and the Structure of Innovation;* Meta Publications, Capitola, Ca., 1991.

Dilts R.; *Changing Belief Systems with NLP;* Meta Publications, Capitola, Ca.,1990.

Dilts, R.; *Applications of NLP;* Meta Publications, Capitola, CA, 1983.

Dilts, R. & Epstein, T.; *Dynamic Learning;* Meta Publications, Capitola, CA, 1995.

Dilts R.; *Strategies of Genius, Volumes I, II & III*; Meta Publications, Capitola, CA, 1994-1995.

Dilts, R. & Zolno, S.; *Skills for the New Paradigm: Lessons from Italy,* ASTD, Spring 1991.

Dilts R.; *NLP and Self-Organization Theory;* Anchor Point, June 1995, Anchor Point Assoc., Salt Lake City, UT.

Dilts R.; *NLP, Self-Organization and Strategies of Change Management;* Anchor Point, July 1995, Anchor Point Associates, Salt Lake City, UT.

Dilts, R., Epstein, T., et al; *Pathways to Leadership* (audio tape series); Dynamic Learning Publications, Ben Lomond, CA, 1991.

Dilts, R. & Epstein, T.; *"NLP in Training Groups";* Dynamic Learning Publications, Ben Lomond, CA, 1989.

Dilts R.; *"NLP in Organizational Development";* OD Network Conference Papers, New York, NY, 1979.

Dilts, R.,*"Let NLP Work for You",* Real Estate Today, February, 1982, Vol. 15, No. 2.

Early, G.; *Negotiations;* I/S S.M. Olsen, Holbaek, Denmark, 1986.

Eicher, J.; *Making the Message Clear: Communicating for Business;* Grinder, DeLozier & Associates, Santa Cruz, CA, 1987.

Gaster, D.; *A Framework For Visionary Leadership,* PACE, Henley-On-Thames, Oxon, England, 1988.

Hersey, P.; *The Situational Leader;* Warner Books, New York, NY, 1984.

Hersey, P. & Blanchard, K.; *Management of Organizational Behavior: Utilizing Human Resources;* Prentice Hall, Englewood Cliffs, NJ, 1969.

Kouzes & Posner; *The Leadership Challenge: How to Get Extraordinary Things Done in Organizations;* Jossey-Bass, San Francisco, CA, 1987.

Laborde, G.; *Influencing With Integrity: Management Skills for Communication and Negotiation;* Syntony Inc., Palo Alto, CA, 1982.

LeBeau, M.; *Negotiation: Winning More Than Money;* Future Pace, San Rafael, CA, 1987.

Maron, D.; *Neuro-Linguistic Programming: The Answer to Change?;* Training and Development Journal, 1979, 33(10), 68.

McMaster, M. & Grinder, J.; *Precision: A New Approach to Communication;* Precision, Los Angeles, CA 1981.

Moine, D.; *"Patterns of Persuasion";* Personal Selling Journal, 1981, 1 (4), 3.

Morgan, G.; *Images of Organization;* Sage Publications, Inc., Beverly Hills, CA, 1986.

Nanus, B.; *Visionary Leadership*; Jossey-Bass, San Francisco, CA, 1992

Nicholls, J.; *Leadership in Organizations: Meta, Macro and Micro;* European Management Journal, 1 Spring 1988.

O'Connor, J., Seymour, J.; *Introducing Neuro-Linguistic Programming;* Aquarian Press, Cornwall, England, 1990.

Pile, S.; *Vision into Action: Creating a Generative Internal Model of Transformational-Transactional Leadership;* Masters Thesis, Pepperdine University, 1988.

Renesch, J. (Ed.); *New Traditions in Business: Spirit and Leadership in the 21st Century*; Sterling & Stone, Inc., San Francisco, CA, 1992.

Richardson, J. & Margoulis; *The Magic of Rapport;* Harbor, San Francisco, CA, 1981.

Schein, E.; *Organizational Culture and Leadership*; Jossey-Bass, San Francisco, CA, 1988.

Sculley, J.; *Odyssey*; Harper & Row, Publishers, San Francisco, CA, 1987.

Senge, P.; *The Fifth Discipline*; Doubleday, New York, NY, 1990.

Smith, S. & Hallbom, T.; *Augmenting the One Minute Manager;* The NLP Connection, Columbus, OH, 1988.

Tichy, N., & Devanna, M. A.; *The Transformational Leader*; John Wiley & Sons, New York, NY, 1986.

Williams, P.; *New Focus in Differentiating Exceptional Leadership: Identifying and Developing the Potential for Organizational Leadership;* OD Network Conference Papers, New York, NY, 1986.

Williams, P.; *Making Leaders Out of Managers;* Northern California Executive Review; August, 1987.

Wheatley, M.; **Leadership and the New Science**; Berrett-Koehler Publishers, Inc., San Francisco, CA., 1992.

Yeager, J.; *Collection of Management Articles Related to NLP;* Eastern NLP Inst., Princeton, NJ, 1985.

Zierden, W.E.; *Leading Through the Follower's Point of View;* Organizational Dynamics; Spring 1980.

Zolno, S.; *Scoring a Place in OD: Skills for Transition;* ASTD, Winter 1992.

Index